Class Diagram: Interfaces

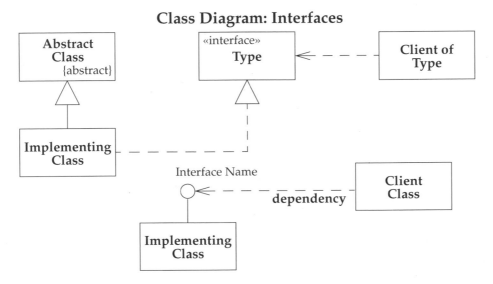

Abstract Class {abstract}

«interface» Type

Client of Type

Implementing Class

Interface Name

dependency

Client Class

Implementing Class

Class Diagram: Parameterized Class

template class

T

Set

bound element

Set<Integer>

Association Class

Class — Class

Association Class

Activity Diagram

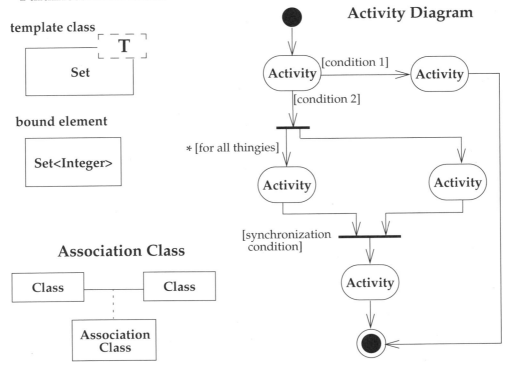

Activity [condition 1] → Activity

[condition 2]

* [for all thingies]

Activity

Activity

[synchronization condition]

Activity

SOFTWARE
Development
PRODUCTIVITY AWARD

UML Distilled is a recipient of the prestigious
1997 *Software Development Magazine Productivity Award*
in the Books category.

Addison Wesley Longman congratulates authors
Martin Fowler and **Kendall Scott**
for their outstanding work.

UML Distilled

Applying the Standard Object Modeling Language

Martin Fowler

with

Kendall Scott

ADDISON-WESLEY

An imprint of Addison Wesley Longman, Inc.
Reading, Massachusetts • Harlow, England • Menlo Park, California
Berkeley, California • Don Mills, Ontario • Sydney
Bonn • Amsterdam • Tokyo • Mexico City

As we prepared for this reprint, the OMG standards group was about to release version 1.2 of the UML. Although I haven't been following every part of this discussion (it is a very specialized topic), I have looked at the issues they have been discussing, and I don't think the planned changes affect the level of detail provided in UML Distilled. *So, I've not needed to make any additional changes to the 1.1 printing to support version 1.2.*

Martin Fowler

Executive Editor: J. Carter Shanklin
Assistant Editor: Angela Buenning
Project Manager: Sarah Weaver
Copyeditor: Arlene Richman
Proofreader: Maine Proofreading Services
Index and Composition: Kendall Scott
Cover Design: Simone Payment

7 8 9 CRS 01 00 99 98
Seventh printing, June 1998

Addison Wesley Longman, Inc., books are available for bulk purchases by corporations, institutions, and other organizations. For more information please contact the Corporate, Government, and Special Sales Department at (800) 238-9682.

The Addison-Wesley Object Technology Series

Grady Booch, Ivar Jacobson, and James Rumbaugh, Series Editors

For more information check out the series web site [http://www.awl.com /cseng/otseries/] as well as the pages on each book [http://www.awl.com/cseng/I-S-B-N/] (I-S-B-N represents the actual ISBN, including dashes).

David Bellin and Susan Suchman Simone,
The CRC Card Book
ISBN 0-201-89535-8

Grady Booch, *Object Solutions: Managing the Object-Oriented Project*
ISBN 0-8053-0594-7

Grady Booch, *Object-Oriented Analysis and Design with Applications, Second Edition*
ISBN 0-8053-5340-2

Don Box, *Essential COM*
ISBN 0-201-63446-5

Alistair Cockburn, *Surviving Object-Oriented Projects: A Manager's Guide*
ISBN 0-201-49834-0

Dave Collins, *Designing Object-Oriented User Interfaces*
ISBN 0-8053-5350-X

Bruce Powel Douglass, *Real-Time UML: Developing Efficient Objects for Embedded Systems*
ISBN 0-201-32579-9

Desmond F. D'Souza and Alan Cameron Wills,
Objects, Components, and Frameworks with UML: The Catalysis Approach
ISBN 0-201-31012-0

Martin Fowler, *Analysis Patterns: Reusable Object Models*
ISBN 0-201-89542-0

Martin Fowler with Kendall Scott, *UML Distilled: Applying the Standard Object Modeling Language*
ISBN 0-201-32563-2

Peter Heinckiens, *Building Scalable Database Applications: Object-Oriented Design, Architectures, and Implementations*
ISBN 0-201-31013-9

Ivar Jacobson, Maria Ericsson, and Agenta Jacobson,
The Object Advantage: Business Process Reengineering with Object Technology
ISBN 0-201-42289-1

Ivar Jacobson, Magnus Christerson, Patrik Jonsson, and Gunnar Overgaard, *Object-Oriented Software Engineering: A Use Case Driven Approach*
ISBN 0-201-54435-0

Ivar Jacobson, Martin Griss, and Patrik Jonsson,
Software Reuse: Architecture, Process and Organization for Business Success
ISBN 0-201-92476-5

David Jordan, *C++ Object Databases: Programming with the ODMG Standard*
ISBN 0-201-63488-0

Wilf LaLonde, *Discovering Smalltalk*
ISBN 0-8053-2720-7

Lockheed Martin Advanced Concepts Center and Rational Software Corporation, *Succeeding with the Booch and OMT Methods: A Practical Approach*
ISBN 0-8053-2279-5

Thomas Mowbray and William Ruh, *Inside CORBA: Distributed Object Standards and Applications*
ISBN 0-201-89540-4

Ira Pohl, *Object-Oriented Programming Using C++, Second Edition*
ISBN 0-201-89550-1

Terry Quatrani, *Visual Modeling with Rational Rose and UML*
ISBN 0-201-61016-3

Yen-Ping Shan and Ralph H. Earle, *Enterprise Computing with Objects: From Client/Server Environments to the Internet*
ISBN 0-201-32566-7

David N. Smith, *IBM Smalltalk: The Language*
ISBN 0-8053-0908-X

Daniel Tkach, Walter Fang, and Andrew So, *Visual Modeling Technique: Object Technology Using Visual Programming*
ISBN 0-8053-2574-3

Daniel Tkach and Richard Puttick, *Object Technology in Application Development, Second Edition*
ISBN 0-201-49833-2

Available Summer/Fall 1998

Grady Booch, James Rumbaugh, and Ivar Jacobson,
Unified Modeling Language User Guide
ISBN 0-201-57168-4

Ivar Jacobson, Grady Booch, and James Rumbaugh,
The Objectory Software Development Process
ISBN 0-201-57169-2

James Rumbaugh, Ivar Jacobson, and Grady Booch,
Unified Modeling Language Reference Manual
ISBN 0-201-30998-X

Contents

Figures

Foreword

When we began to craft the Unified Modeling Language, we hoped that we could produce a standard means of expressing design that would not only reflect the best practices of industry, but would also help demystify the process of software system modeling. We believe that the availability of a standard modeling language will encourage more developers to model their software systems before building them. The benefits of doing so are well-known to the developer community.

The creation of the UML was itself an iterative and incremental process very similar to the modeling of a large software system. The end result is a standard built on, and reflective of, the many ideas and contributions made by numerous individuals and companies from the object community. We began the UML effort, but many others helped bring it to a successful conclusion; we are grateful for their assistance.

Creating and agreeing on a standard modeling language is a significant challenge by itself. Educating the development community, and presenting the UML in a manner that is both accessible and in the context of the software development process, is also a significant challenge. In this deceptively short book, Martin Fowler has more than met this challenge.

In a clear and friendly style, Martin not only introduces the key aspects of UML, but also clearly demonstrates the role UML plays in the development process. Along the way, we are treated to abundant nuggets of modeling insight and wisdom drawn from Martin's 10-plus years of design and modeling experience.

The result is a book we recommend to modelers and developers interested in getting a first look at UML and in gaining a perspective on the key role it plays in the development process.

Grady Booch
Ivar Jacobson
James Rumbaugh

Preface

I never expected to write a methods book.

I was approached to write one late in 1992. By then, however, all the really influential methods books had been published, and I didn't think I had anything significant to add to the literature. As far as I was concerned, the ground was covered—there were better things to do. I had decided not to create a new methodology that was "fowler" than all the others, and there were already too many methodologies.

When Grady Booch, Jim Rumbaugh, and Ivar Jacobson (the "three amigos") joined forces to form a single Unified Modeling Language (UML), I was delighted. Arguments over which method to choose are some of the most tiresome arguments I've had to deal with, particularly since they have little impact on the final result. I was glad to see that argument go away.

When I was approached to write this book, the amigos were beginning to write their books; these books will be the authoritative works on the UML. However, there is a need for a short book to both provide something while the three of them are working on their larger works and act as a concise UML guide. I intended to make this volume the shortest methods book ever written.

Although this is a noble aim for me, is this the right book for you?

I'll start by telling you what this book is *not*.

- It is not a tutorial on OO analysis and design with the UML. The user's guide, led by Grady Booch, will be that book.
- It is not a definitive reference guide to the notation and its semantics. The reference guide, led by Jim Rumbaugh, will be that book.
- It is not a detailed guide to the process of using the UML on object-oriented projects. The process guide, led by Ivar Jacobson, will be that book.

This book is a short guide to the *key parts* of the notation, the semantics, and the process. I am aiming it at those who already have used object technology, probably with one of the many currently available OO analysis and design methods. This book tells you quickly what the key elements of the notation are and what they mean, and it suggests an outline process for using them. I've also taken the opportunity to add tips and suggestions from my use of object methods over the last decade.

Because it is a short book, it will be easier to digest the information and get used to what the UML has to say. It also will provide a good first place to look for reference information.

Chapter 1 looks at what the UML is, the history of its development, and the reasons why you might want to use it.

Chapter 2 discusses the object-oriented development process. Although the UML exists independent of process, I find it hard to discuss modeling techniques without talking about where they fit in with object-oriented development.

Chapters 3 through 10 discuss the various modeling techniques of the UML, in turn. I have organized these chapters around the kinds of diagrams I find useful. I describe the notation, including its semantics, and provide tips about using the techniques. My philosophy is to make clear what the UML says and, at the same time, give you my opinions on how best to use it.

Chapter 11 gives a small example to show how the UML fits in with programming using (of course) Java.

The inside covers summarize the UML notation. You may find it useful to refer to these as you are reading the chapters so that you can check on the notation for the various modeling concepts.

Scattered within the "official UML" chapters are a number of sidebars on other techniques I have found valuable but which are not emphasized in the UML. They certainly can and should be used with the UML.

For each UML and non-UML technique, I've provided summaries about when to use the technique and where to find more information. As I write this, there are no UML books on the market, so I have referenced only pre-UML books. Although the notation is different, many of the concepts are the same, and it will be a while before these books should be relegated to the basement.

Of course, this book, like any book written within our industry, will be out of date as soon as it is finished. To combat this, I'm making the inevitable use of the World Wide Web. To get my latest thoughts on methods, take a look at the Web site for this book: <**www.awl.com/ cseng/titles/0-201-32563-2.html**>.

Acknowledgments

Putting out a book this fast required a lot of help from people who went beyond the normal effort that goes into producing a book to do everything that much more quickly.

Kendall Scott played an important role in pulling together all the material and working over the text and graphics.

The three amigos, Grady Booch, Ivar Jacobson, and Jim Rumbaugh, have been full of support and advice. We have burned up many hours of transcontinental phone calls, and they have improved the book greatly (as well as my understanding of the UML).

A good slate of book reviewers is essential to doing a good job on a book. Not only did these reviewers give me the feedback I needed, they also turned around their comments in less than a week to keep to our tight deadlines. My thanks to: Simmi Kochhar Bhargava of Netscape Communications Corporation, Eric Evans, Tom Hadfield of Evolve Software, Inc., Ronald E. Jeffries, Joshua Kerievsky of Industrial Logic, Inc., Helen Klein of the University of Michigan, James Odell, and Vivek Salgar of Netscape Communications Corporation. Double thanks to Tom Hadfield because he did it twice!

I want to thank Jim Odell for two things: first, for coordinating the Object Management Group (OMG) effort to get a single standard UML, which will be a big step forward for our industry; and second, for encouraging me to get into the object-oriented analysis and design field. Oh, and thanks for reviewing the book, too!

Thanks to Cindy for dealing with me being absent even when I was home.

I can't even imagine the difficulties that my editor, J. Carter Shanklin, and his assistant, Angela Buenning, went through to get this book out as quickly as they did. Whatever these difficulties were, I'm sure Carter and Angela deserve my thanks.

Last, but not least, thanks to my parents for helping me start off with a good education, from which all else springs.

Martin Fowler
Melrose, Massachusetts
May 1997
martin_fowler@compuserve.com

Chapter 1

Introduction

What Is the UML?

The **Unified Modeling Language (UML)** is the successor to the wave of object-oriented analysis and design (OOA&D) methods that appeared in the late '80s and early '90s. It most directly unifies the methods of Booch, Rumbaugh (OMT), and Jacobson, but its reach will be wider than that. As I write this, the UML is in the middle of a standardization process with the OMG (Object Management Group), and I expect it to be the standard modeling language in the future.

The UML is called a modeling language, not a method. Most methods consist, at least in principle, of both a modeling language and a process. The **modeling language** is the (mainly graphical) notation that methods use to express designs. The **process** is their advice on what steps to take in doing a design.

The process parts of many methods books are rather sketchy. Furthermore, I find that most people, when they say they are using a method, use the modeling language, but rarely follow the process. So in many ways, the modeling language is the most important part of the method. It is certainly the key part for communication. If you want to discuss your design with someone, it is the modeling language that both of you need to understand, *not* the process you used to get to that design.

The three amigos are also working on a unified process, which they are going to call Objectory. You don't have to use Objectory in order to use the UML—they are distinctly separate. In this book, however, I talk a little bit about process in order to put the techniques of the modeling language in context. Within this discussion, I use the basic steps and terms of Objectory, but the text is *not* a description of the Objectory process. I find that I use many different processes, depending on my client and on the kind of software I am building. While I think a standard modeling language is valuable, I don't see a comparable need for a standard process, although some harmonization on vocabulary would be useful.

How We Got Here

In the 1980s, objects began to move away from the research labs and took their first steps toward the "real" world. Smalltalk stabilized into a platform that people could use, and C++ was born.

Like many developments in software, objects were driven by programming languages. Many people wondered how design methods would fit into an object-oriented world. Design methods had become very popular in industrial development in the '70s and '80s. Many felt that techniques to help people do good analysis and design were just as important to object-oriented development.

The key books about object-oriented analysis and design methods appeared between 1988 and 1992:

- Sally Shlaer and Steve Mellor wrote a pair of books (1989 and 1991) on analysis and design; the material in these books has evolved into their Recursive Design approach (1997).
- Peter Coad and Ed Yourdon also wrote books that developed Coad's lightweight and prototype-oriented approach to methods. See Coad and Yourdon (1991a and 1991b), Coad and Nicola (1993), and Coad *et al.* (1995).

- The Smalltalk community in Portland, Oregon, came up with Responsibility-Driven Design (Wirfs-Brock *et al.* 1990) and Class-Responsibility-Collaboration (CRC) cards (Beck and Cunningham 1989).

- Grady Booch had done a lot of work with Rational Software in developing Ada systems. His books featured several examples (and the best cartoons in the world of methods books). See Booch (1994 and 1995).

- Jim Rumbaugh led a team at the research labs at General Electric, which came out with a very popular book about a method called Object Modeling Technique (OMT). See Rumbaugh *et al.* (1991) and Rumbaugh (1996).

- Jim Odell based his books (written with James Martin) on his long experience with business information systems and Information Engineering. The result was the most conceptual of these books. See Martin and Odell (1994 and 1996).

- Ivar Jacobson built his books on his experience with telephone switches for Ericsson and introduced the concept of use cases in the first one. See Jacobson (1994 and 1995).

As I prepared to travel to Portland for OOPSLA '94, the methods scene was pretty split and competitive. Each of the aforementioned authors was now informally leading a group of practitioners who liked his ideas. All of these methods were very similar, yet they contained a number of often annoying minor differences among them. The same basic concepts would appear in very different notations, which caused confusion to my clients.

Talk of standardization had surfaced, but nobody seemed willing to do anything about it. Some were opposed to the very idea of standards for methods. Others liked the idea but were not willing to put in any effort. A team from the OMG tried to look at standardization but got only an open letter of protest from all the key methodologists. Grady Booch tried an informal morning coffee approach, with no more success. (This reminds me of an old joke. Question: What is the difference between a methodologist and a terrorist? Answer: You can negotiate with a terrorist.)

For the OO methods community, the big news at OOPSLA '94 was that Jim Rumbaugh had left General Electric to join Grady Booch at Rational Software, with the intention of merging their methods.

The next year was full of amusements.

Grady and Jim proclaimed that "the methods war is over—we won," basically declaring that they were going to achieve standardization the Microsoft way. A number of other methodologists suggested forming an Anti-Booch Coalition.

By OOPSLA '95, Grady and Jim had prepared their first public description of their merged method: version 0.8 of the *Unified Method* documentation. Even more significantly, they announced that Rational Software had bought Objectory, and that Ivar Jacobson would be joining the Unified team. Rational held a party to celebrate the release of the 0.8 draft that was very well-attended. It was also quite a lot of fun, despite Jim Rumbaugh's singing.

During 1996, Grady, Jim, and Ivar, now widely referred to as the three amigos, worked on their method, under its new name: the Unified Modeling Language (UML). However, the other major players in the object methods community were not inclined to let the UML be the last word.

An OMG task force was formed to do standardization in the methods area. This represented a much more serious attempt to address the issues than previous OMG efforts in the methods area. Mary Loomis was given the chair; later Jim Odell joined as co-chair and took over leadership of the effort. Odell made it clear that he was prepared to give up his method to a standard, but he did not want a Rational-imposed standard.

In January 1997, various organizations submitted proposals for a methods standard to facilitate the interchange of models. These proposals focus on a meta-model and an optional notation. Rational released version 1.0 of the UML documentation as their proposal to the OMG.

As I write this, Jim Odell and the OMG group have spent a lot of time working on the semantics of the UML and harmonizing the various submissions. We now have a single UML 1.1 proposal with wide industry support.

Notations and Meta-Models

The UML, in its current state, defines a notation and a meta-model.

The **notation** is the graphical stuff you see in models; it is the syntax of the modeling language. For instance, class diagram notation defines how items and concepts such as class, association, and multiplicity are represented.

Of course, this leads to the question of what exactly is meant by an association or multiplicity or even a class. Common usage suggests some informal definitions, but many people want more rigor than that.

The idea of rigorous specification and design languages is most prevalent in the field of formal methods. In such techniques, designs and specifications are represented using some derivative of predicate calculus. Such definitions are mathematically rigorous and allow no ambiguity. However, the value of these definitions is by no means universal. Even if you can prove that a program satisfies a mathematical specification, there is no way to prove that the mathematical specification actually meets the real requirements of the system.

Design is all about seeing the key issues in the development. Formal methods often lead to getting bogged down in lots of minor details. Also, formal methods are hard to understand and manipulate, often harder to deal with than programming languages. And you can't even execute them.

Most OO methods have very little rigor; their notation appeals to intuition rather than formal definition. On the whole, this does not seem to have done much harm. These methods may be informal, but many people still find them useful—and it is usefulness that counts.

However, OO methods people are looking for ways to improve the rigor of methods without sacrificing their usefulness. One way to do this is to define a **meta-model:** a diagram, usually a class diagram, that defines the notation.

Figure 1-1 is a small piece of the UML 1.1 meta-model that shows the relationship among associations and generalization. (The extract is there just to give you a flavor of what meta-models are like. I'm not even going to try to explain it.)

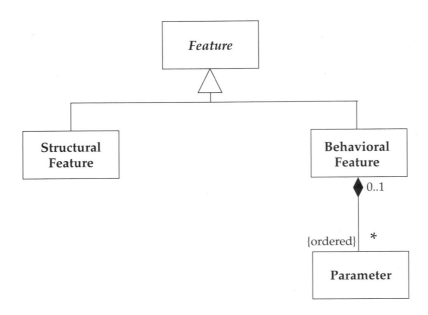

Figure 1-1: *UML 1.1 Meta-Model Extract*

How much does the meta-model affect the user of the modeling notation? Well, it does help define what is a well-formed model—that is,
one that is syntactically correct. As such, a methods power user should
understand the meta-model. However, most users of methods do not
need such deep understanding to get some value out of using the
UML notation.

This is why I was able write a useful book before the UML meta-model
was completely defined. The changes in the meta-model between 1.0
and 1.1 did not cause any major changes to the contents of this book. I
will not be rigorous in this book; rather, I will follow the traditional
methods path and appeal to your intuition.

How strictly should you stick to the modeling language? That
depends on the purpose for which you are using it. If you have a
CASE tool that generates code, then you have to stick to the CASE
tool's interpretation of the modeling language in order to get acceptable code. If you are using the diagrams for communication purposes,
then you have a little more leeway.

If you stray from the official notation, then other developers will not fully understand what you are saying. However, there are times when the official notation can get in the way of your needs. I'll admit that in these cases, I'm not at all afraid to bend the language. I believe that the language should bend to help me communicate, rather than the other way around. But I don't do it often, and I'm always aware that a bend is a bad thing if it causes communication problems. In this book, I mention those places where I'm inclined to do a bit of bending.

Why Do Analysis and Design?

When it comes down to it, the real point of software development is cutting code. Diagrams are, after all, just pretty pictures. No user is going to thank you for pretty pictures; what a user wants is software that executes.

So when you are considering using the UML, it is important to ask yourself why you are doing it and how it will help you when it comes down to writing the code. There's no proper empirical evidence to prove that these techniques are good or bad, but the following subsections discuss the reasons that I often come across for using them.

Learning OO

A lot of people talk about the learning curve associated with OO—the infamous paradigm shift. In some ways, the switch to OO is easy. In other ways, there are a number of obstacles to working with objects, particularly in using them to their best advantage.

It's not that it's difficult to learn how to program in an OO language. The problem is that it takes a while to learn to exploit the advantages that object languages provide. Tom Hadfield puts it well: Object languages *allow* advantages but don't *provide* them. To use these advantages, you have to make the infamous paradigm shift. (Just make sure you are sitting down at the time!)

The techniques in the UML were to some degree designed to help people do good OO, but different techniques have different advantages.

- One of the most valuable techniques for learning OO is CRC cards (see page 64), which are not part of the official UML (although they can and should be used with it). They were designed primarily for teaching people to work with objects. As such, they are deliberately different from traditional design techniques. Their emphasis on responsibilities and their lack of complex notation make them particularly valuable.

- Interaction diagrams (see Chapter 6) are very useful because they make the message structure very explicit and, thus, are useful for highlighting over-centralized designs, in which one object is doing all the work.

- Class diagrams (see Chapters 4 and 5), used to illustrate class models, are both good and bad for learning objects. Class models are comfortably similar to data models; many of the principles that make for a good data model also make for a good class model. The major problem in using class diagrams is that it is easy to develop a class model that is data-oriented rather than being responsibility-oriented.

- The concept of patterns (see page 36) has become vital to learning OO because using patterns gets you to concentrate on good OO designs and to learn by following an example. Once you have gotten the hang of some basic modeling techniques, such as simple class diagrams and interaction diagrams, it is time to start looking at patterns.

- Another important technique is iterative development (see Chapter 2). This technique does not help you learn OO in any direct way, but it is the key to exploiting OO effectively. If you do iterative development from the start, then you will learn, in context, the right kind of process and begin to see why designers suggest doing things the way they do.

When you start using a technique, you tend to do it by the book. My recommendation is to begin with the simple notations that I talk about here, particularly with class diagrams. As you get comfortable, you can pick up the more advanced ideas as you need them. You may also find you wish to extend the method.

The UML has an extension mechanism that uses stereotypes. I talk about stereotypes only in the context of class diagrams, but you can use stereotypes with any diagram to extend its meaning. The three amigos' books will go into more detail on that. Just make sure you really understand what the construct means. Toward that end, I like to look at any construct from three perspectives: conceptual, specification, and implementation (see Chapter 4).

Communicating with Domain Experts

One of our biggest challenges in development is that of building the *right* system—one that meets users' needs at a reasonable cost. This is made more difficult because we, with our jargon, have to communicate with users, who have their own, more arcane, jargon. (I did a lot of work in health care, and there the jargon isn't even in English!) Achieving good communication, along with good understanding of the users' world, is the key to developing good software.

The obvious technique to use in addressing this is use cases (see Chapter 3). A **use case** is a snapshot of one aspect of your system. The sum of all use cases is the external picture of your system, which goes a long way toward explaining what the system will do.

A good collection of use cases is central to understanding what your users want. Use cases also present a good vehicle for project planning, because they control iterative development, which is itself a valuable technique since it gives regular feedback to the users about where the software is going.

While use cases help with communication about surface things, it is also crucial to look at the deeper things. This involves learning how your domain experts understand their world.

Class diagrams (see Chapters 4 and 5) can be extremely valuable here, as long as you use them in a *conceptual* manner. In other words, you should treat each class as a concept in a user's mind, part of his or her language. The class diagrams you draw are then not diagrams of data or of classes, but diagrams of the language of your users. James Martin and Jim Odell's "foundations" book (1994) is a good source for this kind of thinking with class diagrams.

I have found activity diagrams (see Chapter 9) to be very useful in cases in which workflow processes are an important part of the users' world. Since activity diagrams support parallel processes, they can help you get away from unnecessary sequences. The way these diagrams de-emphasize the links to classes, which can be a problem in later design, becomes an advantage during this more conceptual stage of the development process.

Understanding the Big Picture

As a consultant, I often have to breeze into a complex project and look intelligent in a very short period of time. I find the design techniques I discuss above invaluable for that because they help me acquire an overall view of the system. A look at a class diagram can quickly tell me what kinds of abstractions are present in the system and where the questionable parts are that need further work. As I probe deeper, I want to see how classes collaborate, so I ask to see interaction diagrams that illustrate key behaviors in the system.

If this is useful to me as an outsider, it is just as useful to the regular project team. It's easy to lose sight of the forest for the trees on a large project. With a few choice diagrams in hand, you can find your way around the software much more easily.

To build a road map, use package diagrams (see Chapter 7) at the higher levels to scope out a class diagram. When you draw a class diagram for a road map, take a specification perspective. It is very important to hide implementations with this kind of work. Don't document every interaction; instead, focus on the key ones.

Use patterns (see page 36) to describe the key ideas in the system; they help you to explain why your design is the way it is. It is also useful to describe designs you have rejected and why you rejected them. I always end up forgetting that kind of decision.

Looking for More Information

This book is not a complete and definitive reference to the UML, let alone OO analysis and design. There are a lot of words out there and a lot of worthwhile things to read. As I discuss the individual topics, I will talk about other books you should go to for more in-depth information on the ideas in the UML and on OOA&D in general.

Of course, your first step beyond this book should be the three amigos' books on the UML. As I write this, they are planning three books, each of which will be led by one of the three.

Grady Booch is leading the work on the user's guide. This will be a tutorial book that will contain a number of in-depth case studies on how to use the UML on practical problems. It will go into more detail than this book and give more advice on how to use the UML well.

Jim Rumbaugh is leading the effort on the reference book, the definitive guide to the UML's notation and meta-model. It will be the final source of information about what the UML means when it says something.

Ivar Jacobson is working on a book that will describe the process of using the UML. Strictly speaking, the UML is a modeling language and does not contain anything about the process you use to develop software. That is why the amigos use the term "modeling language" and not "method," since a method should properly include a process. I have outlined a lightweight process in this book to give the techniques and the notation some context. Jacobson's book will go into more detail.

Of course, the three amigos' books are not the only books you should read to learn about good OOA&D. My list of recommended books changes frequently; take a look at the *Survey of Analysis and Design Methods* page at my Web site for the most current version, reachable from <**ourworld.compuserve.com/homepages/Martin_Fowler**> (my home page).

In particular, I suggest reading books on patterns for material that will take you beyond the basics. Now that the methods war is over, I think that patterns will be where most of the interesting material about analysis and design will appear. Inevitably, however, people will come up with new analysis and design techniques, and it is likely that they will talk about how these techniques can be used with the UML. This is another benefit of the UML; it encourages people to add new techniques without duplicating work that everyone else has done.

Chapter 2

An Outline Development Process

The UML is a modeling language, not a method. The UML has no notion of process, which is an important part of a method.

The three amigos are working on merging their processes. The result will be called the *Rational Objectory Process*. I don't believe you can have a single process for software development. Various factors associated with software development lead you to different kinds of process. These factors include the kind of software you are developing (real-time, information system, desktop product), the scale (single developer, small team, 100-plus-member team), and so forth. So, the amigos are trying to come up with a process framework, something that will capture the common elements but still give people the latitude to use techniques that are appropriate for their project.

The title of this book is *UML Distilled*, so I could have safely ignored process. However, I don't believe that modeling techniques make any sense without knowing how they fit into a process.

I think it's important to discuss the process first so that you can see how an object-oriented development works. I won't go into great detail on the process; I will provide just enough to give you a sense of the typical way in which a project that uses these techniques is run.

As I discuss the outline process, I will use the terminology and outline framework of Objectory. (I have to use something, and that seems as good as anything.) I have not tried to describe Objectory; that is beyond the scope of this book. Rather, I'm describing a lightweight, low-ceremony process that is consistent with Objectory. For full details on Objectory, you should go to the amigos' process book.

Although the Objectory process contains details about what kinds of models to develop at the various stages in the process, I won't go into such details. Nor will I specify tasks, deliverables, and roles. My terminology is looser than that of Objectory—that is the price one pays for lightweight description.

Whatever process discussion there is, don't forget that you can use *any* process with the UML. The UML is independent of process. You should pick something that is appropriate for your kind of project. Whatever process you use, you can use the UML to record the resulting analysis and design decisions.

Overview of the Process

Figure 2-1 shows the high-level view of the development process.

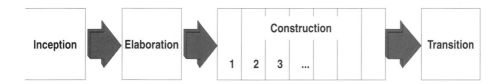

Figure 2-1: *Outline Development Process*

This process is an iterative and incremental development process, in that the software is not released in one big bang at the end of the project but is, instead, developed and released in pieces. The **construction** phase consists of many **iterations**, in which each iteration builds production-quality software, tested and integrated, that satisfies a subset of the requirements of the project. The delivery may be external, to early users, or purely internal. Each iteration contains all the usual life-cycle phases of analysis, design, implementation, and testing.

In principle, you can start at the beginning: Pick some functionality and build it, pick some other functionality, and so forth. However, it is worthwhile to spend some time planning.

The first two phases are inception and elaboration. During **inception**, you establish the business rationale for the project and decide on the scope of the project. This is where you get the commitment from the project sponsor to go further. In **elaboration**, you collect more detailed requirements, do high-level analysis and design to establish a baseline architecture, and create the plan for construction.

Even with this kind of iterative process, there is some work that has to be left to the end, in the **transition** phase. This can include beta testing, performance tuning, and user training.

Projects vary in how much **ceremony** they have. High-ceremony projects have a lot of formal paper deliverables, formal meetings, formal sign-offs. Low-ceremony projects might have an inception phase that consists of an hour's chat with the project's sponsor and a plan that sits on a spreadsheet. Naturally, the bigger the project, the more ceremony you need. The fundamentals of the phases still occur, but in very different ways.

I try to keep the ceremony to a minimum, and my discussion reflects that. There will be plenty of high-ceremony processes to choose from elsewhere.

I've shown iterations in the construction phase, but not in the other phases. In fact, you can have iterations in all phases, and it is often a good idea to do so in a large phase. Construction is the key phase in which to iterate, however.

That's the high-level view. Now we will delve into the details so that we have enough information to see where the techniques discussed later in the book fit into the larger scheme of things. In doing this, I will talk a bit about these techniques and when to use them. You may find it a little confusing if you are unfamiliar with the techniques. If that's the case, skip those bits and come back to them later.

Inception

Inception can take many forms. For some projects, it's a chat at the coffee machine: "Have a look at putting our catalog of services on the Web." For bigger projects, it might be a full-fledged feasibility study that takes months.

During the inception phase, you work out the business case for the project—roughly how much it will cost and how much it will bring in. You will also need to get a sense of the project's scope. You may need to do some initial analysis to get a sense of the size of the project.

I don't tend to make a big deal of inception. Inception should be a few days' work to consider if it is worth doing a few months' worth of deeper investigation during elaboration (see below). At this point, the project's sponsor agrees to no more than a serious look at the project.

Elaboration

So you have the go-ahead to start a project. At this stage, typically, you have only a vague idea of the requirements. For instance, you might be able to say:

> *We are going to build the next-generation customer support system for the Watts Galore Utility Company. We intend to use object-oriented technology to build a more flexible system that is more customer-oriented—specifically, one that will support consolidated customer bills.*

Of course, your requirements document will likely be more expansive than that, but it may not actually say very much more.

At this point, you want to get a better understanding of the problem.

- What is it you are actually going to build?
- How are you going to build it?
- What technology are you going to use?

In deciding what issues to look into during this phase, you need to be driven, first and foremost, by the risks in your project. What are the things that could derail you? The bigger the risk, the more attention you have to pay to it.

In my experience, risks can usefully be classified into four categories:

1. *Requirements risks.* What are the requirements of the system? The big danger is that you will build the wrong system, one that does not do what the customer wants it to do. During the elaboration phase, you need to get a good handle on the requirements and their relative priorities.

2. *Technological risks.* What are the technological risks you have to face? Ask yourself these questions.

   a. You are going to use objects. Have you much experience doing OO design work?

   b. You have been told to use Java and the Web. How well does this technology work? Can you actually deliver the functions that users need through a Web browser connected to a database?

3. *Skills risks.* Can you get the staff and expertise you need?

4. *Political risks.* Are there political forces that can get in the way and seriously affect your project?

There may be more in your case, but risks that fall into these four categories are nearly always present.

Dealing with Requirements Risks

Requirements are important and are where UML techniques can most obviously be brought to bear. The starting point is use cases. Use cases drive the whole development process.

Use cases are discussed in detail in Chapter 3; I will just give you a brief description here of what use cases are.

A use case is a typical interaction that a user has with the system in order to achieve some goal. Imagine the word processor that I am currently using. One use case would be "make selected text bold"; another would be "create an index for a document."

As you can see from these examples, use cases can vary considerably in size. The key is that each one indicates a function that the user can understand and that has value for that user. A developer can respond with specifics.

> *It will take me two months to do the index function for you. I also have a use case to support grammar checking. I have time to do only one—which would you like first? If you want bold text, I can do that in a week, and I can do italics at the same time.*

Use cases provide the basis of communication between sponsors and developers in planning the project.

One of the most important things to do in the elaboration phase is to discover all the potential use cases for the system you are building. In practice, of course, you aren't going to get all of them. You want to get most, however, particularly the most important ones. It's for this reason that, during the elaboration phase, you should schedule interviews with users for the purpose of gathering use cases.

Use cases do not need to be detailed. I usually find a paragraph or three of descriptive text is sufficient. This text should be specific enough for the users to understand the basic idea and for the developers to have a broad sense of what lurks inside.

Use cases are not the whole picture, however. Another important task is to come up with the skeleton of a conceptual model of the domain. Within the heads of one or more users lies a picture of how the business operates. For instance:

> *Our customers may have several sites, and we provide several services to these sites. At the moment, a customer gets a bill for all services at a given site. We want that customer to be billed for all services at all sites. We call this consolidated billing.*

This passage contains the words "customer," "site," and "service." What do these terms mean? How do they fit together? A conceptual domain model starts to answer these questions and, at the same time, lays the foundation for the object model that will be used to represent the objects in the system later in the process. I use the term **domain model** to describe any model whose primary subject is the world that the computer system is supporting, whatever stage of the development process you are in.

In Objectory, you use different models to capture different aspects of development. Domain models and use cases capture functional requirements; analysis models explore the implications of these requirements for a particular application; design models add the internal infrastructure to make the application work. Objectory's domain model is mostly built before you find any use cases; its purpose is to explore the vocabulary of the domain in terms that are meaningful to the domain experts.

After you have a domain model and a use case model, you develop a **design model** that realizes both the information in the domain objects and the behavior in the use cases. The design model adds classes to actually do the work and also to provide a reusable architecture for future extensions. In larger projects, you may develop an intermediate analysis model to explore the consequences of the external requirements before making design decisions.

Objectory does not require you to construct the entire system in a "waterfall" manner. It is important to get the key domain classes and key use cases correct and then to build a reusable system architecture that will support future extensions. Then, additional uses cases can be added incrementally, and they can be implemented in the design model as part of an iterative development process. The whole system should not be built in one "big bang."

I find two UML techniques particularly valuable in building domain models.

- Class diagrams, when drawn from a conceptual perspective (see Chapter 4), are great for capturing the language of the business. You can use these diagrams to lay out the concepts that the business experts use as they think about the business and to lay out the ways those experts link concepts together.

- Activity diagrams (see Chapter 9) complement class diagrams by describing the workflow of the business—that is, the steps people go through in doing their jobs. The key aspect of activity diagrams is that they encourage finding parallel processes, which is important in eliminating unnecessary sequences in business processes.

Some people like to use interaction diagrams (see Chapter 6) to explore how various roles interact in the business. By thinking about workers and activities together, they find it easier to gain an understanding of the process. I prefer to use activity diagrams to figure out what needs to be done first and to address who does what later.

Interaction diagrams are more useful during that later step. Also, interaction diagrams don't encourage parallel processes in the way activity diagrams do. You can use activity diagrams with swimlanes to deal with both people and parallelism, but it does make the diagrams more complicated. (You can also use state diagrams [see Chapter 8] in conjunction with workflow, but I find them more awkward to use in that context.)

Domain modeling can be a great adjunct to use cases. When I gather use cases, I like to bring in a domain expert and explore how that person thinks about the business, with the help of conceptual class diagrams and activity diagrams.

In this situation, I use minimal notation, I don't worry about rigor, and I make lots of informational notes on the diagram. I don't try to capture every detail. Instead, I focus on important issues and areas that imply risk. I draw lots of unconnected diagrams without worrying about consistency and interrelationships among diagrams.

I find that this process can quickly yield a lot of understanding. Armed with this understanding, I find that I can more easily identify the use cases for the different users.

After I've covered most of the relevant areas, I like to consolidate the different diagrams into a single consistent domain model. For this, I use one or two domain experts who like to get deeper into the modeling. I maintain a conceptual perspective but, at the same time, become more rigorous.

I try to develop a single domain model that will support all the requirements expressed in the earlier discrete models. This model can then act as a starting point for building classes and a deeper class design in the construction phase. If this model is large, I use packages to divide the model into chunks. I'll do consolidation for class and activity diagrams and perhaps draw a couple of state diagrams for classes that have interesting lifecycles.

You should think of the initial domain model as a skeleton, not as a high-level model. The term "high-level model" implies that a lot of details are missing. I have seen this mistake made in several situations, expressed as, for instance, "Don't show attributes on these models." The results are models with no substance. It's easy to see why developers deride such efforts.

You can't take the opposite approach and build a detailed model, however. If you do, it will take ages and you will die from analysis paralysis. The trick is to find and concentrate on the important details. Most of the details will be dealt with during iterative development. This is why I prefer to think of this model as a skeleton. The skeleton is the foundation of the rest of the model. It is detailed, but it is only a small part of the story.

Naturally, this does not tell you how to differentiate bone from flesh; that is the art of the skilled analyst, and I haven't figured out how to bottle that yet!

Domain modeling is also driven by the use cases as they become known. As use cases appear, the modeling team should look at them to assess whether they contain anything that could have a strong impact on the domain model. If so, they should explore further; if not, the use cases should be put aside for the time being.

The team that builds the domain model should be a small group (two to four people) that includes developers and domain experts. The smallest viable team would be one developer and one domain expert. The domain expert (and preferably the developer, too) should be trained in how to use the appropriate UML diagrams for conceptual modeling.

The team should work intensively during the elaboration period until it reaches closure on the model. During this period, the leadership should ensure that the team neither gets bogged down in details nor operates at so high a level that their feet don't touch the ground. Once they get the hang of what they are doing, bogging down is the biggest danger. A hard deadline works well in concentrating minds.

As part of understanding the requirements, you should build a prototype of any tricky parts of the use cases. Prototyping is a valuable technique for getting a better understanding of how more dynamic situations work. Sometimes, I can feel I understand the situation well from the diagrams, but there are other times when I feel I really need a prototype to get a proper feel for what's going on. Usually, I don't prototype the whole picture but, instead, use the overall domain model to highlight areas that do need prototyping.

When you use a prototype, don't be constrained by the environment in which you will actually deliver. I have often gained a lot from analysis prototyping in Smalltalk, even if I am building a C++ system.

Dealing with Technological Risks

The most important thing to do in addressing technological risks is to build prototypes that try out the pieces of technology you are thinking of using.

For example, say you are using C++ and a relational database. These are the steps you should follow:

1. Get the C++ compilers and other tools.
2. Build a simple part of an early version of the domain model. See how the tools work for you.
3. Build the database and connect it to the C++ code.
4. Try several tools. See which ones are easiest to work with and best suited for the job. Get comfortable with the tools you choose.

Don't forget that the biggest technological risks are inherent in how the components of a design fit together, rather than present in any of the components themselves. You may know C++ well, and you may know relational databases well, but putting them together is not so easy. This is why it is very important to get all the components you intend to use and fit them together at this early stage of the process.

You should also address any architectural design decisions during this stage. These usually take the form of ideas of what the major components are and how they will be built. This is particularly important if you are contemplating a distributed system.

As part of this exercise, focus on any areas that look like they will be difficult to change later. Try to do your design in a way that will allow you to change elements of the design relatively easily. Ask yourself these questions.

- What will happen if a piece of technology doesn't work?
- What if we can't connect two pieces of the puzzle?
- What is the likelihood of something going wrong? How would we cope if that happens?

As with the domain model, you should look at the use cases as they appear in order to assess if they contain anything that could cripple your design. If you fear they may contain a "purple worm," investigate further.

During this process, you will typically use a number of UML techniques to sketch out your ideas and document the things you try. Don't try to be comprehensive at this point; brief sketches are all you need and, therefore, all you should use.

- Class diagrams (see Chapters 4 and 5) and interaction diagrams (see Chapter 6) are useful in showing how components communicate.
- Package diagrams (see Chapter 7) can show a high-level picture of the components at this stage.
- Deployment diagrams (see Chapter 10) can provide an overview of how pieces are distributed.

Dealing with Skills Risks

I often go to conferences and listen to case-study talks given by people who have just done an object-oriented project. They usually answer the question: "What were your biggest mistakes?" with responses that always include "We should have gotten more training."

It never ceases to amaze me how companies embark on important OO projects with little experience and little thought to how to gain more.

People worry about the costs of training, but they pay every penny as the project takes longer.

Training is a way to avoid making mistakes because instructors have already made those mistakes. Making mistakes takes time, and time costs money. So you pay the same either way, but not having the training causes the project to take longer.

I'm not a big fan of formal training courses. I've taught many of them and designed some as well. I remain unconvinced that they are effective in teaching object-oriented skills. They give people an overview of what they need to know, but they don't really pass on the core skills that you need to do a serious project. A short training course can be useful, but it's only a beginning.

If you do go for a short training course, pay a lot of attention to the instructor. It is worth paying a lot extra for someone who is knowledgeable and entertaining because you will learn a lot more in the process. Also, get your training in small chunks, just at the time you need it. If you don't apply what you have learned in a training course straight away, you will forget it.

The best way to acquire OO skills is through **mentoring**, in which you have an experienced developer work with your project for an extended period of time. The mentor shows you how to do things, watches what you do, and passes on tips and short bits of training.

A mentor will work with the specifics of your project and knows which bits of expertise to apply at the right time. In the early stages, a mentor is one of the team, helping you come up with a solution. As time goes on, you become more capable and the mentor does more reviewing than doing. My goal as a mentor is to render myself unnecessary.

You can find mentors for specific areas or for the overall project. Mentors can be full time or part time. Many mentors like to work a week out of each month on each project; others find that too little. Look for a mentor with knowledge and the ability to transfer that knowledge. Your mentor may be the most important factor in your project's success; it is worth paying for quality.

If you can't get a mentor, consider a project review every couple of months or so. Under this setup, an experienced mentor comes in for a few days to review various aspects of the design. During this time, the reviewer can highlight any areas of concern, suggest additional ideas, and outline any useful techniques that the team may be unaware of. Although this does not give you the full benefits of a good mentor, it can be valuable in spotting key things that you can do better.

You can also supplement your skills by reading. Try to read a solid technical book at least once every other month. Even better, read it as part of a book group. Find a couple of other people who want to read the same book. Agree to read a few chapters a week, and spend an hour or two discussing those chapters with the others. By doing this, you can gain a better understanding of the book than by reading it on your own. If you are a manager, encourage this. Get a room for the group; give your staff the money to buy technical books; allocate time for a book group.

The patterns community has found book groups to be particularly valuable. Several patterns reading groups have appeared. Look at the patterns home page (<**http://st-www.cs.uiuc.edu/users/patterns/patterns.html**>) for more information about these groups.

As you work through elaboration, keep an eye out for any areas in which you have no skills or experience. Plan to acquire the experience at the point at which you need it.

Dealing with Political Risks

I can't offer you any serious advice on this because I'm not a skilled corporate politician. I strongly suggest that you find someone who is.

Baseline Architecture

An important result of elaboration is that you have a **baseline architecture** for your system. This architecture consists of

- Your list of use cases, which tells you what the requirements are
- Your domain model, which captures your understanding of the business and serves as the starting point for your key domain classes
- Your technology platform, which describes the key pieces of implementation technology and how they fit together

This architecture is the foundation of your development; it acts as the blueprint for later stages. Inevitably, the details of the architecture will change, but it shouldn't sustain too many serious changes.

The importance of a stable architecture does vary with your technology, however. In Smalltalk, you can make significant architectural changes much more easily because of the rapid edit-run cycle times and the lack of strong typing. This allows architecture to be very evolutionary, as illustrated by the *Episodes* process pattern (see Cunningham 1996). In C++, it is more important to have a stable architecture that underpins construction.

When Is Elaboration Finished?

My rule of thumb is that elaboration takes about a fifth of the total length of the project. Two events are key indicators that elaboration is complete:

- The developers can feel comfortable providing estimates, to the nearest person-week of effort, of how long it will take to build each use case.
- All the significant risks have been identified, and the major ones are understood to the extent that you know how you intend to deal with them.

Planning

The essence of a plan is to set up a series of iterations for construction and to assign use cases to iterations.

The plan is finished when each use case is put into an iteration and each iteration's start date has been identified. The plan isn't more detailed than that.

The first step is to categorize the use cases.

- The users should indicate the level of priority for each use case. I usually use three levels.
  —"I absolutely must have this function for any real system."
  —"I can live without this function for a short period."

—"It's an important function, but I can survive without it for a while."

- The developers should consider the **architectural risk** associated with each use case, which is the risk that if the use case is put aside until late in the project, the work that has gone before will be significantly compromised, resulting in a lot of rework. Again, I tend to use three categories: high risk, possible but not likely, and little chance.

- The developers should assess how confident they feel about estimating the effort required for each use case. I refer to this as the **schedule risk**. I find three levels useful here, as well.

  — "I'm pretty sure I know how long it will take."

  — "I can estimate the time only to the nearest person-month."

  — "I have no idea."

Once this is done, you should estimate the length of time each use case will require, to the nearest person-week. In performing this estimate, assume you need to do analysis, design, coding, unit testing, integration, and documentation. Assume also that you have a fully committed developer with no distractions (we'll add a fudge factor later).

Note that I believe that the *developers* should estimate, *not* the managers. In keeping with that idea, you should ensure that the developer with the most knowledge of a given use case does the estimate.

Once your estimates are in place, you can assess whether you are ready to make the plan. Look at the use cases with high schedule risk. If a lot of the project's time is tied up in these use cases or if these use cases contain a lot of architectural risk, then you need to do more elaboration.

The next step is to determine your iteration length. You want a fixed iteration length for the whole project so that you get a regular rhythm to the iteration delivery. An iteration should be long enough for you to do a handful of use cases. For Smalltalk, it can be as low as two to three weeks, for instance; for C++, it can be as high as six to eight weeks.

Now you can consider how much effort you have for each iteration.

A good place to start is to assume your developers will operate at an average of 50% efficiency—half their time will be spent on developing use cases. Multiply the length of the iteration by the number of developers by one-half. The result is how much development effort you have for each iteration. For instance, given eight developers and a three–week iteration length, you would have 12 developer-weeks (8 * 3 * 1/2) of effort per iteration.

Add up your time for all use cases, divide by the effort per iteration, and add one for luck. The result is your first estimate of how many iterations you will need for your project.

The next step is to assign the use cases to iterations.

Use cases that carry high priority, architectural risk, and/or schedule risk should be dealt with early. Do *not* put off risk until the end! You may need to split big use cases, and you will probably revise use case estimates in light of the order in which you are doing things. You can have less work to do than the effort in the iteration, but you should never schedule more than your effort allows.

For transition, allocate from 10% to 35% of the construction time for tuning and packaging for the delivery. (Use a higher figure if you are inexperienced with tuning and packaging in your current environment.)

Then add a contingency factor: 10% to 20% of the construction time, depending on how risky things look. Add this factor to the end of the transition phase. You should plan to deliver without using contingency time—that is, on your internal target date—but commit to deliver at the end of contingent time.

After following all these guidelines, you should have a plan that shows the use cases that will be done during each iteration. This plan symbolizes commitment among developers and users; a good name for this plan is the **commitment schedule.** This schedule is not cast in stone—indeed, everyone should expect the commitment schedule to change as the project proceeds. Since it is a commitment between developers and users, however, changes must be made jointly.

As you can see from this discussion, use cases serve as the foundation for planning the project, which is why the UML puts a lot of emphasis on them.

Construction

Construction builds the system in a series of iterations. Each iteration is a mini-project. You do analysis, design, coding, testing, and integration for the use cases assigned to each iteration. You finish the iteration with a demo to the user and perform system tests to confirm that the use cases have been built correctly.

The purpose of this process is to reduce risk. Risk often appears because difficult issues are left to the end of the project. I have seen projects in which testing and integration are left to the end. Testing and integration are big tasks, and they always take longer than people think.

Back in the days of OS/360, Fred Brooks estimated that half a given project was testing (and the inevitable bug fixing). Testing and integration are more difficult when left to the end—and more demoralizing.

All this effort leads to a big risk. With iterative development, you do the whole process for every iteration, which gets you into the habit of coping with all the issues each time.

The older I get, the more aggressive I get about testing. I like Kent Beck's rule of thumb that a developer should write at least as much test code as production code. Testing should be a continuous process. No code should be written until you know how to test it. Once you have written it, write the tests for it. Until the tests work, you cannot claim to have finished writing the code.

Test code, once written, should be kept forever. Set up your test code so that you can run every test with a simple command line or GUI button push. The code should respond either with "OK" or with a list of failures. Also, all tests should check their own results. There is nothing more time-wasting than having a test output a number, the meaning of which you have to research.

Separate the tests into unit and system tests. Unit tests should be written by the developers. They should be organized on a package basis and coded to test the interfaces of all classes. System tests should be developed by a separate small team whose only job is testing. This team should take a black-box view of the system and take particular delight in finding bugs. (Sinister mustaches and cackling laughs are optional but desirable.)

The iterations within construction are both incremental and iterative.

- The iterations are *incremental* in function. Each iteration builds on the use cases developed in the previous iterations.

- They are *iterative* in terms of the code base. Each iteration will involve rewriting some existing code to make it more flexible. **Refactoring** (see sidebar) is a highly useful technique in iterating the code. It's a good idea to keep an eye on the amount of code thrown away in each iteration. Be suspicious if less than 10% of the previous code is discarded each time.

Refactoring

Have you come across the principle of software entropy? It suggests that programs start off in a well-designed state, but as new bits of functionality are tacked on, programs gradually lose their structure, eventually deforming into a mass of spaghetti.

Part of this is due to scale. You write a small program that does a specific job well. People ask you to enhance the program, and it gets more complex. Even if you try to keep track of the design, this can still happen.

One of the reasons that software entropy occurs is that when you add a new function to a program, you build on top of the existing program, often in a way the existing program was not intended to support. In such a situation, you can either redesign the existing program to better support your changes or you can work around those changes in your additions.

Although in theory it is better to redesign your program, this usually results in extra work because any rewriting of your existing program will introduce new bugs and problems. Remember the old engineering adage: "If it ain't broke, don't fix it!" However, if you don't redesign your program, the additions will be more complex than they should be.

Gradually, this extra complexity will exact a stiff penalty. Therefore, there is a trade-off: Redesigning causes short-term pain for longer-term gain. Schedule pressure being what it is, most people prefer to put their pain off to the future.

Refactoring is a term used to describe techniques that reduce the short-term pain of redesigning. When you refactor, you do not change the functionality of your program; rather, you change its internal structure in order to make it easier to understand and work with.

Refactoring changes are usually small steps: renaming a method, moving a field from one class to another, consolidating two similar methods into a superclass. Each step is tiny, yet a couple of hours' worth of performing these small steps can do a world of good to a program.

Refactoring is made easier by the following principles:

- Do not refactor a program and add functionality to it at the same time. Impose a clear separation between the two when you work. You might swap between them in short steps—for instance, half an hour refactoring, an hour adding a new function, and half an hour refactoring the code you just added.

- Make sure you have good tests in place before you begin refactoring. Run the tests as often as possible. That way, you will know quickly if your changes have broken anything.

- Take short, deliberate steps. Move a field from one class to another. Fuse two similar methods into a superclass. Refactoring often involves making many localized changes that result in a larger-scale change. If you keep your steps small and test after each step, you will avoid prolonged debugging.

You should refactor when

- You add functionality to your program and you find the old code getting in the way. When that becomes a problem, stop adding the new function and, instead, refactor the old code.

- You have difficulty understanding the code. Refactoring is a good way of helping you understand the code and preserving that understanding for the future.

You will often find you want to refactor code that someone else wrote. When you do this, do it alongside the code's author. It is difficult to write code in a way that others can easily understand. The best way to refactor is to work alongside someone who does understand the code. Then you can combine her understanding with your unfamiliarity.

When to Use Refactoring

Refactoring is a much underused technique. It has only begun to be recognized, mainly in the Smalltalk community. However, I believe it is a key technique in improving software development, regardless of your environment. Ensure that you understand how to do refactoring in a disciplined way. One way to do this is to have your mentor teach you the techniques.

Where to Find Out More

Because refactoring is still a new technique, little has been written about it. William Opdyke's Ph.D. thesis (1992) is probably the most extensive treatment of the subject, but it is geared to automatic refactoring tools rather than techniques that humans can use now. Kent Beck is one of the foremost exponents of refactoring; his patterns book (1996) includes many patterns that are central to refactoring. See also Beck's 1997 article, which gives a good flavor of the process of refactoring.

If you use VisualWorks or IBM Smalltalk, you should download Refactory, a tool that supports refactoring (see <**http://st-www.cs. uiuc.edu/users/droberts/Refactory.html**>). This tool was developed by Don Roberts and John Brant, who work with Ralph Johnson at the University of Illinois. I believe that this tool is the most important development in coding tools since the Integrated Development Environment.

Integration should be a continuous process. For starters, full integration is part of the end of each iteration. However, integration can and should occur more frequently than that. A developer should integrate after every significant piece of work. The full suite of unit tests should be run at each integration to ensure full regression testing.

Iterative Development and Planning

Within each iteration, you can also do more detailed planning. A key part of any plan is coping with things that are not going according to plan. Let's face it; it always happens.

The key feature of iterative development is that it is time-boxed—you are not allowed to slip any dates. Instead, use cases can be moved to a later iteration via negotiation and agreement with the sponsor. The point of this is to maintain a regular habit of hitting dates and to avoid the bad habit of slipping dates.

Note, however, that if you find yourself deferring too many use cases, it's time to redo the plan, including reestimating use case effort levels. By this stage, the developers should have a better idea of how long things will take.

Using the UML in Construction

All UML techniques are useful during this stage. Since I am going to refer to techniques I haven't had a chance to talk about yet, feel free to skip this section and come back to it later.

As you look to add a given use case, you first use the use case to determine what your scope is. A conceptual class diagram (see Chapter 4) can be useful to rough out some concepts for the use case and see how these concepts fit with the software that has already been built. If the use case contains significant workflow elements, you can look at those with an activity diagram (see Chapter 9).

The advantage of these techniques at this stage is that they can be used in conjunction with the domain expert. As Brad Kain says: Analysis occurs only when the domain expert is in the room (otherwise it is pseudo-analysis).

I have found that for the move to design, a specification-perspective class diagram (see Chapter 4) can be useful in mapping out the classes in more detail. Interaction diagrams (see Chapter 6) are valuable to show how the classes will interact to implement the use case.

You can try to draw the class and interaction diagrams directly or use CRC cards (see page 64) to explore the behavior, and then document with diagrams, if you wish. Regardless of which approach you take, I believe it is important to pay a lot of attention to responsibilities in this stage of the work.

I find UML diagrams useful for getting an overall understanding of a system. In doing this, however, I should stress that I do not believe in producing detailed diagrams of the whole system. To quote Ward Cunningham (1996):

> *Carefully selected and well-written memos can easily substitute for traditional comprehensive design documentation. The latter rarely shines except in isolated spots. Elevate those spots...and forget about the rest.*

Confine your documentation to the areas in which the documentation helps. If you find the documentation isn't helping you, it's a sign that something is going wrong.

I use a package diagram (see Chapter 7) as my logical road map of the system. This diagram helps me understand the logical pieces of the system and see the dependencies (and keep them under control).

I like to use tools to help me identify the dependencies and to make sure I don't miss them. Even simple tools such as Perl scripts can help here. Java, with its explicit support for packages, is a great help. A deployment diagram (see Chapter 10), which shows the high-level physical picture, may also prove useful at this stage.

Within each package, I like to see a specification-perspective class diagram. I don't show every operation on every class. I show only the associations and key attributes and operations that help me understand what is in there.

This class diagram acts as a graphical table of contents. Often, it helps to keep a glossary of classes that contains brief definitions of each class, often via statements of responsibilities. It is also a good idea to keep responsibility statements in the code as comments and extract them with a suitable tool.

If a class has complex lifecycle behavior, I draw a state diagram (see Chapter 8) to describe it. I do this only if the behavior is sufficiently complex, which I find doesn't happen often. More common are complicated interactions among classes, for which I produce an interaction diagram.

My favorite form of documentation has three basic elements.

1. One or two pages describing a few classes in a class diagram
2. A few interaction diagrams showing how the classes collaborate
3. Some text to pull the diagrams together

Often I include some important code, written in a literate program style. If there is a particularly complex algorithm involved, I'll consider using an activity diagram (see Chapter 9), but only if it gives me more understanding than the code alone. In these cases, I use a specification-perspective or implementation-perspective class diagram or perhaps both—it depends on what I'm trying to communicate.

In Objectory, you should draw interaction diagrams (see Chapter 7) for every use case you identify. These interaction diagrams should cover every scenario. You don't need a separate diagram for each scenario, but you should ensure that the logic of every scenario is captured by the interaction diagram that addresses the associated use case. For more information on the details of Objectory, see the amigos' process book.

If I find concepts that are coming up repeatedly, I use patterns (see sidebar) to capture the basic ideas.

I use patterns in a number of ways; I also tend to use various forms of patterns. A pervasive design pattern would suggest the use of a Gang of Four–style pattern (see Gamma *et al.* 1994). However, I use other forms as well, depending on what best seems to fit a particular situation. (As you might expect, I keep a particular eye out for analysis patterns—see Fowler 1997.)

Patterns are useful within the scope of a project and also in communicating good ideas outside the project. Indeed, I see patterns as particularly valuable for cross-project communication, as well.

Patterns

The UML tells you how to express an object-oriented design. **Patterns** look, instead, at the results of the process: example models.

Many people have commented that projects have problems because the people involved were not aware of designs that are well-known to those with more experience. Patterns describe common ways of doing things. They are collected by people who spot repeating themes in designs. These people take each theme and describe it so that other people can read the pattern and see how to apply it.

Let's look at an example. Say you have some objects running in a process on your desktop, and they need to communicate with other objects running in another process. Perhaps this process is also on your desktop; perhaps it resides elsewhere. You don't want the objects in your system to have to worry about finding other objects on the network or executing remote procedure calls.

What you can do is create a *proxy* object within your local process for the remote object. The proxy has the same interface as the remote object. Your local objects talk to the proxy using the usual in-process message sends. The proxy then is responsible for passing any messages on to the real object, wherever it might reside.

Figure 2-2 is a class diagram (see Chapter 4) that illustrates the structure of the *Proxy* pattern.

Proxies are a common technique used in networks and elsewhere.

People have a lot of experience using proxies in terms of knowing how they can be used, what advantages they can bring, their limitations, and how to implement them. Methods books like this one don't discuss this knowledge; all they discuss is how you can diagram a proxy. Although useful, it is not as useful as discussing the experience involving proxies.

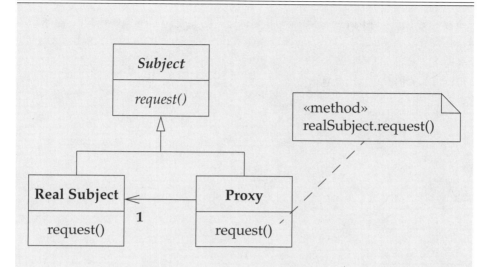

Figure 2-2: *Proxy Design Pattern*

In the early 1990s, some people began to capture this experience. They formed a community interested in writing patterns. These people sponsor conferences and have produced several books.

The most famous patterns book to emerge from this group is the Gang of Four book (Gamma *et al.* 1994), which discusses 23 design patterns in detail.

If you want to know about proxies, this is the source. The Gang of Four book spends 10 pages on the subject, giving details about how the objects work together, the benefits and limitations of the pattern, common variations and usages, and implementation tips for Smalltalk and C++.

Proxy is a design pattern because it describes a design technique. Patterns can also exist in other areas. Say you are designing a system for managing risk in financial markets. You need to understand how the value of a portfolio of stocks changes over time. You could do this by keeping a price for each stock and time-stamping the price. However, you also want to be able to consider the risk in hypothetical situations (for instance, "What will happen if the price of oil collapses?").

To do this, you can create a *Scenario* that contains a whole set of prices for stocks. Then you can have separate *Scenarios* for the prices last week, your best guess for next week, your guess for next week if oil prices collapse, and so forth. This *Scenario* pattern (see Figure 2-3) is an analysis pattern because it describes a piece of domain modeling.

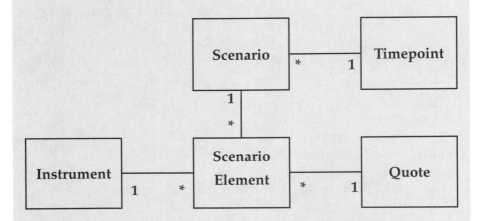

Figure 2-3: *Scenario Analysis Pattern*

Analysis patterns are valuable because they give you a better start when you work with a new domain. I started collecting analysis patterns because I was frustrated by new domains. I knew I wasn't the first person to model them, yet each time I had to start with a blank sheet of paper.

The interesting thing about analysis patterns is they crop up in unusual places. When I started working on a project to do corporate financial analysis, I was enormously helped by a set of patterns I had previously discovered in health care.

See Fowler (1997) to learn more about *Scenario* and other analysis patterns.

A pattern is much more than a model. A pattern must also include the reason why it is the way it is. It is often said that a pattern is a solution to a problem. The pattern must make the problem clear, explain why it solves the problem, and also explain in what circumstances it works and does not work.

Patterns are important because they are the next stage beyond understanding the basics of a language or a modeling technique. Patterns give you a series of solutions and also show you what makes a good model and how you go about constructing a model. They teach by example.

When I started out, I wondered why I had to invent things from scratch. Why didn't I have handbooks to show me how to do common things? The patterns community is trying to build these handbooks.

When to Use Patterns

Patterns should be used all the time. Whenever you try to develop something in analysis, design, coding, or project management, you should search for any available patterns that might help you.

Where to Find Out More

At the moment, the patterns field is still young, so there is not much material (which is a relief in a way since the patterns community has not figured out how to index the material yet!).

The central source of information on patterns is the Patterns Home Page on the Web: <**http://st-www.cs.uiuc.edu/users/patterns/patterns.html**>. This gives you key information about books, conferences, and the like. A number of patterns and information about them are kept at Ward Cunningham's Portland Patterns Repository page: <**http://c2.com/ppr/index.html**>.

The most influential book on patterns is Gamma *et al.* (1994), which is a book of design patterns. You can also find design patterns in Buschmann (1996), together with higher-level architectural patterns. These discuss how such things as pipes and filters, blackboard architectures, and reflection work. At a lower level, you can find books, such as Kent Beck's on Smalltalk patterns (1996), on patterns for specific programming languages. Many of Beck's patterns are good for other languages, as well. For domain modeling, I have to suggest my book (Fowler 1997) on analysis patterns.

The patterns community has regular Pattern Languages of Programming (PLoP) conferences, which are designed to help patterns writers. Selected patterns from these conferences are published in the PLoPD series of books (Coplien and Schmidt 1995 and Vlissides *et al.* 1996), which include many valuable papers.

The UML includes some notation to describe the use of a design pattern. I don't go into it here as it is still in its early stages of usage, but you will find more about it in the three amigos' books.

Transition

The point of iterative development is to do the whole development process regularly so that the development team gets used to delivering finished code. But there are some things that should not be done early. A prime example is optimization.

Optimization reduces the clarity and extensibility of the system in order to improve performance. That is a trade-off you need to make—after all, a system does have to be fast enough to meet users' requirements. But optimizing too early makes development tougher, so this is one thing that does need to be left to the end.

During transition, there is no development to add functionality (unless it is small and absolutely essential). There *is* development to fix bugs.

A good example of a transition phase is that time between the beta release and the final release of a product.

When to Use Iterative Development

You should use iterative development only on projects that you want to succeed.

Perhaps that's a bit glib, but as I get older, I get more aggressive about using iterative development. Done well, it is an essential technique, which you can use to expose risk early and to obtain better control over development. It is not the same as having no management (although, to be fair, I should point out that some have used it that way). It does need to be well-planned. But it is a solid approach, and every OO development book encourages using it—for good reason.

Where to Find Out More

The obvious starting point is the three amigos' process book.

My favorite sources include Goldberg and Rubin (1995), Booch (1994), McConnell (1996), and Graham (1993).

- Goldberg and Rubin talk a lot about general principles and cover a lot of ground.
- Booch's book is more directed. It says what he does, and it offers lots of advice and rules of thumb.
- McConnell also presents plenty of advice, much of it tailored to the kind of process described in this chapter.
- If you want a step-by-step, fully defined methodology for iterative development, the best material I have seen is in Graham's book.

Rational Software has an unpublished description of the current version of the Objectory process as a product. In published books, the closest description comes in Jacobson (1994 and 1995). You should also take a look at the patterns papers contained in Coplien and Schmidt (1995), and at Ward Cunningham's "episodes" paper (1996).

Kent Beck is working on a book of project management patterns. When it comes out, it will doubtless be an excellent resource. In fact, many ideas in this chapter come from conversations with him and Ward Cunningham, as well as from phone conversations with Ivar Jacobson.

Chapter 3

Use Cases

Use cases are interesting phenomena. For a long time, in both object-oriented and traditional development, people used typical scenarios to help them understand requirements. However, these scenarios were treated very informally—always done but rarely documented. Ivar Jacobson is well-known for changing this with his Objectory method and associated book (his first one).

Jacobson raised the visibility of the use case (his name for a scenario) to the extent that it became a primary element in project development and planning. Since his book was published (1994), the object community has adopted use cases to a remarkable degree. My practice has certainly improved since I started using use cases in this manner.

So what is a use case?

In essence, a **use case** is a typical interaction between a user and a computer system. Take the word processor I'm using to write this book. Two typical use cases would be "make some text bold" and "create an index." From just those examples, you can get a sense for a number of properties of use cases.

- A use case captures some user-visible function.
- A use case may be small or large.
- A use case achieves a discrete goal for the user.

In its simplest usage, you capture a use case by talking to your typical users and discussing the various things they might want to do with the system. Take each discrete thing they want to do, give it a name, and write up a short textual description (no more than a few paragraphs).

During elaboration, this is all you need to get started. Don't try to capture all the details right at the start—you can get them when you need them. If you think that a given use case has major architectural ramifications, however, you will need more details up front. Most use cases can be detailed during the given iteration as you build them.

User Goals and System Interactions

An important issue I've come across with use cases is the difference between what I call user goals and system interactions. For example, consider the style sheet functionality found in most word processors.

With **system interactions**, you can say that the use cases would include the likes of "define a style," "change a style," and "move a style from one document to another." However, all these use cases reflect things the user is doing with the system rather than the real goals the user is trying to achieve. The real **user goals** might be described with terms like "ensure consistent formatting for a document" and "make one document's format the same as another."

This dichotomy between user goal and system interaction is not present in all situations. For example, the process of indexing a document is pretty much the same whether you think of it as a user goal or a system interaction. However, where user goals and system interactions do differ, it is important to be aware of the difference.

Both styles of use cases have their applications. System interaction use cases are better for planning purposes; thinking about user goals is important so that you can consider alternative ways to satisfy the goals. If you rush too quickly toward system interaction, you will miss out on creative ways to satisfy user goals more effectively than you might by using the obvious first choice. In each case it is a good idea to ask yourself, "Why did we do that?" That question usually leads to a better understanding of the user goal.

In my work, I focus on user goals first, and then I come up with use cases to satisfy them. By the end of the elaboration period, I expect to have at least one set of system interaction use cases for each user goal I have identified (at minimum, for the user goals I intend to support in the first delivery).

Use Case Diagrams

In addition to introducing use cases as primary elements in software development, Jacobson (1994) also introduced a diagram for visualizing use cases. The **use case diagram** is also now part of the UML.

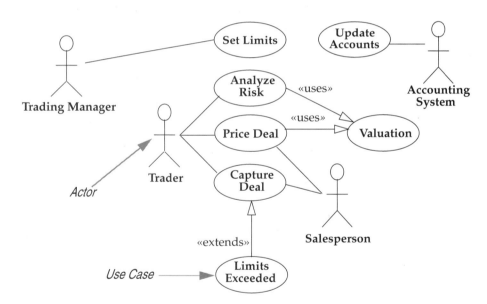

Figure 3-1: *Use Case Diagram*

Figure 3-1 shows some of the use cases for a financial trading system.

I'll begin discussion of the elements of this diagram by talking about the actors.

Actors

An **actor** is a role that a user plays with respect to the system. There are four actors in Figure 3-1: Trading Manager, Trader, Salesperson, and Accounting System.

There will probably be many traders in the given organization, but as far as the system is concerned, they all play the same role. A user may also play more than one role. For instance, one senior trader may play the Trading Manager role and also be a regular trader; a Trader may also be a Salesperson. When dealing with actors, it is important to think about roles rather than people or job titles.

Actors carry out use cases. A single actor may perform many use cases; conversely, a use case may have several actors performing it.

In practice, I find that actors are most useful when trying to come up with the use cases. Faced with a big system, it can often be difficult to come up with a list of use cases. It is easier in those situations to arrive at the list of actors first, and then try to work out the use cases for each actor.

Note that actors don't need to be human, even though actors are represented as stick figures within a use case diagram. An actor can also be an external system that needs some information from the current system. In Figure 3-1, we can see the need to update the accounts for the Accounting System.

The subject of interactions with external systems causes a lot of confusion and stylistic variations among users of use case diagrams.

1. Some people feel that all interactions with remote systems need to be shown on the diagram. For example, if you need access to Reuters in order to price a deal, you should show a link between the Price Deal use case and Reuters.

2. Some feel that you should only show external-interaction use cases when it is the other system that initiates the contact. Using this rule, you would show only the use case for the Accounting System if that system invokes some process to tell the source system to do that.

3. Some feel that you should show system actors only when they are the ones who need the use case. So if the system generates a file every night that is subsequently picked up by the Accounting System, then Accounting System is the relevant actor because it is the one that needs the file produced.

4. Some feel that thinking of a system as an actor is the wrong focus. Instead, they deem an actor is a user who wants something from the system (for example, a particular file). In the case of our example system, the actors would be the internal auditors of the company.

All things considered, I lean toward option 3.

Use cases are all about externally-required functionality. If the Accounting System needs a file, that is a requirement that needs to be satisfied.

Accessing Reuters is important but not a user need. If you follow option 4, you end up analyzing the Accounting System, which is something you would probably rather not get into. That said, you should always question use cases with system actors, find out what the real user goals are, and consider alternative ways of meeting those goals.

When I'm working with actors and use cases, I don't worry too much about what the exact relationships are among them. Most of the time, what I'm really after is the use cases; the actors are just a way to get there. As long as I get all the use cases, I'm not worried about the details of the actors.

One situation in which the actors do live on, however, is in configuring the system for different kinds of users. If your system has use cases that correspond with high-level user functions, you can use the actor/use case links to profile individual users. Each user would have an associated list of actor names, which you would use to determine which use cases that user can perform.

Another good reason to track the actors involves needing to know who wants which use case. This can be important when you are assessing competing needs. Understanding the actors may help you negotiate among competing development demands. They can also be useful in specifying security policy.

Some use cases don't have clear links to specific actors. Consider a utility company. Clearly, one of its use cases is "send out bill." It's not so easy to identify an associated actor, however. No particular user role requests a bill. The bill is sent to the customer, but the customer wouldn't object if it didn't happen. The best guess at an actor here is the Billing Department, in that it gets value from the use case. But Billing is not usually involved in playing out the use case.

Actors can have various roles with regard to a use case. They can be the ones that get value from the use case, or they can just participate in the use case. Depending on how you use the actor relationship, different actor roles will be important to you. I tend to be most concerned with controlling system development. So I'm generally most interested in who wants a given use case to be built—usually those people who get value from the use case.

The key is to remain aware that some use cases will not pop out as a result of the process of thinking about the use cases for each actor. If that happens, don't worry too much. The important thing is understanding the use cases and the user goals they satisfy.

A good source for identifying use cases is external events. Think about all the events from the outside world to which you want to react. A given event may cause a system reaction that does not involve users, or it may cause a reaction primarily from the users. Identifying the events that you need to react to will help you identify the use cases.

Uses and Extends

In addition to the links among actors and use cases, there are two other types of links in Figure 3-1. These represent the uses and extends relationships among use cases. These are often the source of confusion for people who get the purposes of these two verbs confused, so take a moment to understand them.

You use the **extends** relationship when you have one use case that is similar to another use case but does a bit more.

In our example, the basic use case is Capture Deal. This is the case in which all goes smoothly. There are things that can upset the smooth capture of a deal, however. One of these things is when some limit is exceeded—for instance, the maximum amount the trading organization has established for a particular customer. Here we don't perform the usual behavior associated with the given use case; we carry out a variation.

We could put this variation within the Capture Deal use case. However, this would clutter that use case with a lot of special logic, which would obscure the "normal" flow.

Another way to address the variation is to put the normal behavior in one use case and the unusual behavior somewhere else. The following is the essence of the extends relationship.

1. Capture the simple, normal use case first.
2. For every step in that use case, ask "What could go wrong here?" and "How might this work out differently?"
3. Plot all variations as extensions of the given use case. There will often be a fairly high number of extensions. Listing them separately makes things much easier to understand.

You may find that you do use case splitting in both the elaboration and construction phases. In elaboration, I often split any use case that's getting too complicated. However, there are use cases whose full complexity I don't get into until construction.

I split at the construction stage of the project if I can't build the whole use case in one iteration. I split a complex use case into a normal case and a few extensions and then build the normal case in one iteration and the extensions as part of one or more later iterations. (This will result in a change of the commitment schedule, of course, and needs to be negotiated with the users.)

The **uses** relationship occurs when you have a chunk of behavior that is similar across more than one use case and you don't want to keep copying the description of that behavior. For instance, both Analyze Risk and Price Deal require you to value the deal. Describing deal valuation involves a fair chunk of writing, and I hate copy-and-paste operations. So I spun off a separate Value Deal use case for this situation and referred to it from the original use cases.

Note the similarities and differences between extends and uses. Both of them imply factoring out common behavior from several use cases to a single use case that is used, or extended by, several other use cases. However, the *intent* is different.

The two types of relationships imply different things in their links to actors. In the case of extends, actors have a relationship to the use case that is being extended. It is assumed that a given actor will perform both the base use case and all of the extensions. With a uses relationship, there is often no actor associated with the common use case. Even if there is, that actor is not considered to be performing the other use cases.

Apply the following rules.

- Use extends when you are describing a variation on normal behavior.
- Use uses when you are repeating yourself in two or more separate use cases and you want to avoid repetition.

You may hear the term **scenario** in connection with use cases. This word is used inconsistently. Sometimes, scenario is used as a synonym for use case. Within the UML, scenario refers to a single path through a use case, one that shows a particular combination of conditions within that use case. For example, if we want to order some goods, we would have a single use case with several associated scenarios: one in which all goes well; one in which there are not enough goods; one in which our credit is refused; and so forth.

As you perform your modeling tasks, you will come up with models that express how to do your use cases, either in software or in people (that is, squishyware). Obviously, there is more than one way to carry out a use case. In UML-speak, we say that a use case can have many **realizations**.

Often, you may want to sketch out several realizations to discuss before you decide which one to go with. If you do this, always remember to keep notes about discarded realizations, including why you discarded them. I don't want to tell you how many hours I have wasted in discussions that featured the likes of "I *know* there was a reason why we didn't do that…."

When to Use Use Cases

I can't imagine a situation now in which I would not use use cases. They are an essential tool in requirements capture and in planning and controlling an iterative project. Capturing use cases is one of the primary tasks of the elaboration phase—in fact, it is the first thing you should do.

Most of your use cases will be generated during that phase of the project, but you will uncover more as you proceed. Keep an eye out for them at all times. Every use case is a potential requirement, and until you have captured a requirement, you cannot plan to deal with it.

Some people list and discuss the use cases first, then do some modeling. I sometimes do that, but I've also found that conceptual modeling with users helps uncover use cases. I recommend that you try it both ways and see which works best for you.

Different designers make use of use cases with varying degrees of granularity. For example, Ivar Jacobson says that for a 10-person-year project, he would expect about 20 use cases (not counting uses and extends relationships). In a recent project of about the same magnitude, I had more than 100 use cases. I prefer smaller-grained use cases because they make it easier to work with the commitment schedule. However, too many use cases can be overwhelming. I don't think there is one right answer at the moment, so be flexible and work with whatever seems comfortable.

Where to Find Out More

I think the world is still waiting for a really good book on use cases. Naturally, Jacobson's first book (1994) is a source, given that it's the book that started the ball rolling. Jacobson's follow-up book (1995) is useful for its accent on business process use cases (which arguably should be used all the time). Ian Graham (1993) also includes some good advice (he uses the term "script" in place of "use case"). You should also look at the papers on use cases at Alistair Cockburn's Web site: <**http://members.aol.com/acockburn**>.

Chapter 4

Class Diagrams:
The Essentials

The class diagram technique has become truly central within object-oriented methods. Virtually every method has included some variation on this technique.

In addition to being widely used, the class diagram is also subject to the greatest range of modeling concepts. Although the basic elements are needed by everyone, the advanced concepts are used less often. Therefore, I've broken my discussion of class diagrams into two parts, the essentials (this chapter) and the advanced (see Chapter 5).

A **class diagram** describes the types of objects in the system and the various kinds of static relationships that exist among them. There are two principal kinds of static relationships:

- **associations** (for example, a customer may rent a number of videos)
- **subtypes** (a nurse is a kind of person)

Class diagrams also show the attributes and operations of a class and the constraints that apply to the way objects are connected.

The various OO methods use different (and often conflicting) terminology for these concepts. This is extremely frustrating but inevitable, given that OO languages are just as inconsiderate. It is in this area that the UML will bring some of its greatest benefits in simplifying these different diagrams.

Figure 4-1 shows a typical class diagram.

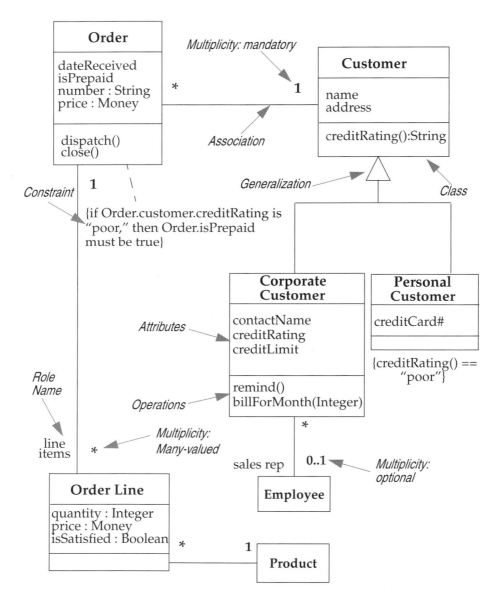

Figure 4-1: *Class Diagram*

Perspectives

Before I begin describing class diagrams, I would like to bring out an important subtlety in the way people use them. This subtlety is usually undocumented but has an impact on the way you should interpret a diagram, for it very much concerns what it is you are describing with a model.

Following the lead of Steve Cook and John Daniels (1994), I say that there are three perspectives you can use in drawing class diagrams (or indeed any model, but this breakdown is most noticeable in connection with class diagrams).

- **Conceptual**. If you take the conceptual perspective, you draw a diagram that represents the concepts in the domain under study. These concepts will naturally relate to the classes that implement them, but there is often no direct mapping. Indeed, a conceptual model should be drawn with little or no regard for the software that might implement it, so it can be considered language-independent. (Cook and Daniels call this the essential perspective; I use the term "conceptual" because it has been around for a long time.)

- **Specification**. Now we are looking at software, but we are looking at the interfaces of the software, not the implementation. We are thus looking at types rather than classes. Object-oriented development puts a great emphasis on the difference between interface and implementation, but this is often overlooked in practice because the notion of class in an OO language combines both interface and implementation. So you often hear the interfaces referred to as types and the implementation of those interfaces as the classes. Most methods, influenced by the language treatment, have followed suit. This is changing (Java and CORBA will have some influence here), but not quickly enough. A type represents an interface that may have many implementations, different because of, say, implementation environment, performance characteristics, or vendor. The distinction can be very important in a number of design techniques based on delegation; see the discussion of this topic in Gamma *et al.* (1994).

- **Implementation**. In this view, we really do have classes and we are laying the implementation bare. This is probably the most often-used perspective, but in many ways the specification perspective is often a better one to take.

Understanding perspective is crucial to both drawing and reading class diagrams. Unfortunately, the lines between the perspectives are not sharp, and most modelers do not take care to get their perspective sorted out when they are drawing. As I talk about class diagrams further, I will stress how each element of the technique depends heavily on the perspective.

When you draw a diagram, draw it from a single, clear perspective. When you read a diagram, make sure you know from which perspective it has been drawn. That knowledge is essential if you are to interpret the diagram properly.

Perspective is not part of the formal UML, but I have found it extremely valuable when modeling and when reviewing models. The UML can be used with all three perspectives. By tagging classes with a stereotype (see page 75), you can provide an indication of the perspective. You mark classes with «implementation class» to show implementation perspective and «type» for specification and conceptual perspectives. Most users of OO methods take an implementation perspective, which is a shame because the other perspectives are often more useful.

Table 4-1 lists four UML terms that appear in Figure 4-1 and their corresponding terms within other well-established methodologies.

Associations

Figure 4-1 shows a simple class model that would not surprise anyone who has worked with order processing. I'll describe each of the pieces and talk about how you would interpret them from the various perspectives.

I'll begin with the associations. **Associations** represent relationships between instances of classes (a person works for a company; a company has a number of offices).

Table 4-1: *Class Diagram Terminology*

UML	Class	Association	Generalization	Aggregation
Booch	Class	Has	Inherits	Containing
Coad	Class & Object	Instance Connection	Gen-Spec	Part-Whole
Jacobson	Object	Acquaintance Association	Inherits	Consists of
Odell	Object Type	Relationship	Subtype	Composition
Rumbaugh	Class	Association	Generalization	Aggregation
Shlaer/ Mellor	Object	Relationship	Subtype	N/A

From the **conceptual** perspective, associations represent conceptual relationships between classes. The diagram indicates that an Order has to come from a single Customer and that a Customer may make several Orders over time. Each of these Orders has several Order Lines, each of which refers to a single Product.

Each association has two **roles**; each role is a direction on the association. Thus, the association between Customer and Order contains two roles: one from Customer to Order; the second from Order to Customer.

A role can be explicitly named with a label. In this case, the role in the direction Order to Order Lines is called Line Items. If there is no label, you name a role after the target class—so the role from Order to Customer would be called Customer. (In this book, I refer to the class that the role goes from as the **source** and the class the role goes to as the **target**. This means that there is a Customer role whose source is Order and whose target is Customer.)

A role also has **multiplicity**, which is an indication of how many objects may participate in the given relationship. In Figure 4-1, the * between Customer and Order indicates that a Customer may have many Orders associated with it; the **1** indicates that an Order comes from only one Customer.

In general, the multiplicity indicates lower and upper bounds for the participating objects. The * actually represents the range *0..infinity*: a Customer need not have placed an Order, and there is no upper limit (in theory, at least!) to the number of Orders a Customer may place. The **1** stands for *1..1*: an Order must have been placed by exactly one Customer.

The most common multiplicities in practice are 1, *, and 0..1 (you can have either none or one). For a more general multiplicity, you can have a single number (such as *11* for players on a cricket team), a range (such as *2..4* for players of a canasta game), or discrete combinations of numbers and ranges (such as *2, 4* for doors in a car).

Figure 4-2 shows cardinality notations in the UML and the major pre-UML methods.

Within the **specification** perspective, associations represent responsibilities.

Figure 4-1 implies that there are one or more methods associated with Customer that will tell me what orders a given Customer has made. Similarly, there are methods within Order that will let me know which Customer placed a given Order and what Line Items comprise an Order.

If there are standard conventions for naming query methods, I can probably infer from the diagram what these methods are called. For example, I may have a convention that says that single-valued relationships are implemented with a method that returns the related object and multi-valued relationships are implemented with an enumeration (iterator) into a collection of the related objects.

Working with a naming convention like this in Java, for instance, I can infer the following interface for an Order class:

```
class Order {

    public Customer customer();

    //Enumeration of order lines
    public Enumeration orderLines();
```

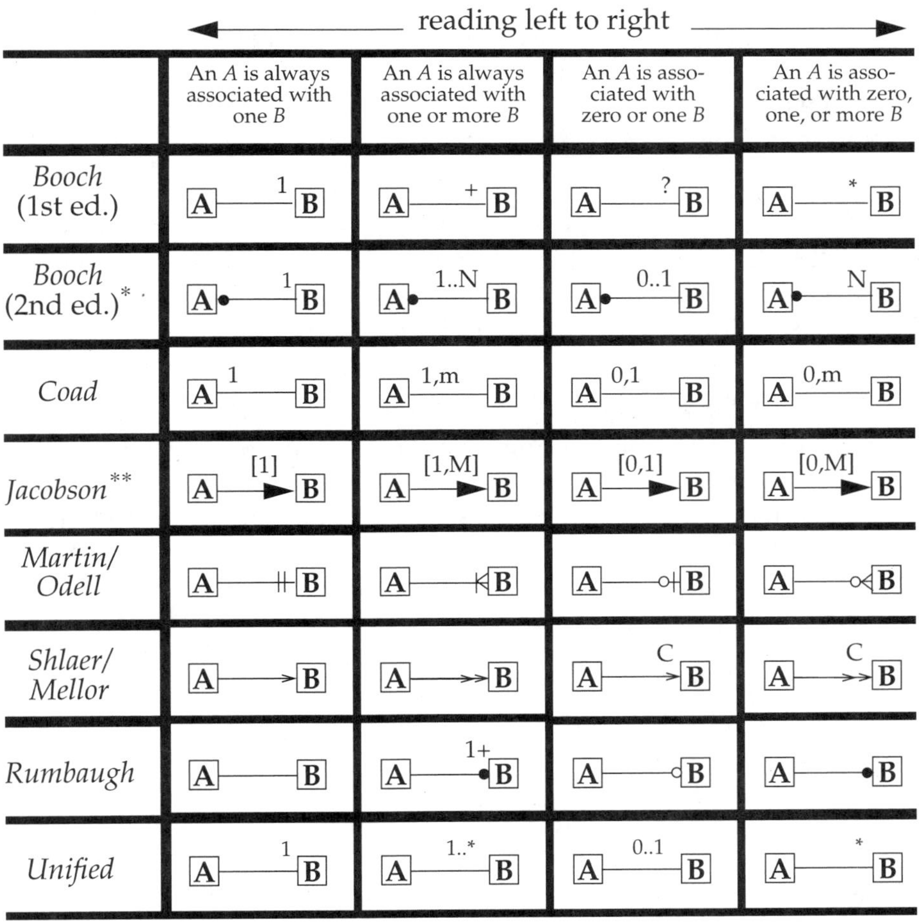

reading left to right

	An *A* is always associated with one *B*	An *A* is always associated with one or more *B*	An *A* is associated with zero or one *B*	An *A* is associated with zero, one, or more *B*
Booch (1st ed.)	A —^{1}— B	A —$^+$— B	A —$^?$— B	A —*— B
Booch (2nd ed.)[*]	A•—^{1}— B	A•—$^{1..N}$— B	A•—$^{0..1}$— B	A•—^{N}— B
Coad	A^1— B	A^{1,m}— B	A^{0,1}— B	A^{0,m}— B
Jacobson[**]	A—$^{[1]}$→ B	A—$^{[1,M]}$→ B	A—$^{[0,1]}$→ B	A—$^{[0,M]}$→ B
Martin/ Odell	A —⊩ B	A —◁ B	A —○ B	A —○◁ B
Shlaer/ Mellor	A —→ B	A —↠ B	A —^{C}→ B	A —^{C}↠ B
Rumbaugh	A — B	A —$^{1+}$• B	A —○ B	A —• B
Unified	A —^{1}— B	A —$^{1..*}$— B	A —$^{0..1}$— B	A —*— B

[*] may be unidirectional
[**] unidirectional

Figure 4-2: *Cardinality Notations*

Obviously, programming conventions will vary from place to place and will not indicate every method, but they can be very useful in finding your way around.

Figure 4-1 also implies some responsibility for updating the relationship. There should be some way of relating the Order to the Customer. Again, the details are not shown; it could be that you specify the Customer in the constructor for the Order. Or, perhaps there is an *addOrder* method associated with Customer. You can make this more explicit by adding operations to the class box (as we will see later).

These responsibilities do *not* imply data structure, however. From a specification-level diagram, I can make no assumptions about the data structure of the classes. I cannot and should not be able to tell whether the Order class actually contains a pointer to Customer, or whether the Order class fulfills its responsibility by executing some selection code that asks each Customer if it refers to a given Order. The diagram indicates only the interface—nothing more.

If this were an **implementation** model, we would now imply that there are pointers in both directions between the related classes. The diagram would now say that Order has a field that is a collection of pointers to Order Lines and also has a pointer to Customer. In Java, we could infer something like the following:

```
class Order {
        private Customer _customer;
        private Vector _orderLines;
class Customer {
        private Vector _orders;
```

In this case, we cannot infer anything from the associations about the interface. The operations on the class would give us this information.

Now take a look at Figure 4-3. It is basically the same as Figure 4-1 except that I have added a couple of arrows on the association lines. These arrows indicate **navigability**.

In a specification model, this would indicate that an Order has a responsibility to tell you which Customer it is for, but a Customer has no corresponding ability to tell you which Orders it has. Instead of symmetrical responsibilities, we now have responsibilities on only one side of the line. In an implementation diagram, one would indicate that Order contains a pointer to Customer but Customer would not point to Order.

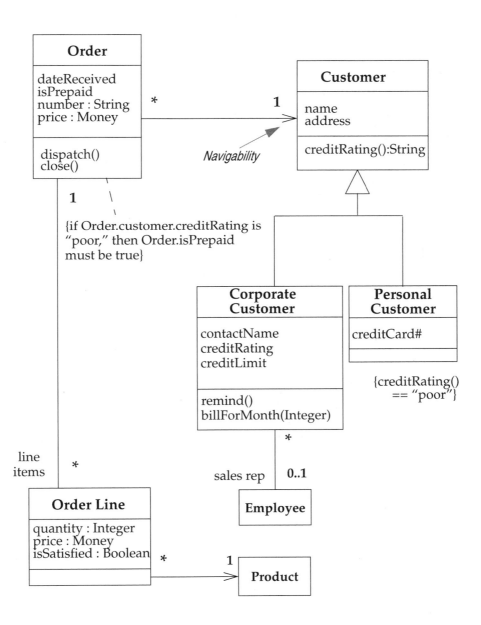

Figure 4-3: *Class Diagram with Navigabilities*

As you can see, navigability is an important part of implementation and specification diagrams. I don't think navigability serves any useful purpose on conceptual diagrams, however.

You will often see a conceptual diagram that first appears with no navigabilities. Then the navigabilities are added as part of the shift to the specification and implementation perspectives. Note also that the navigabilities are likely to be different between specification and implementation.

If a navigability exists in only one direction, we call the association a **uni-directional association**. A **bi-directional association** contains navigabilities in both directions. The UML says that you treat associations without arrows to mean either the navigability is unknown or the association is bi-directional. Your project should settle on one or the other meaning. I prefer it to mean "undecided" for specification and implementation models.

Bi-directional associations include an extra constraint, which is that the two roles are inverses of each other. This is similar to the notion of inverse functions in math. In the context of Figure 4-3, this means that every Line Item associated with an Order must be associated with the original Order. Similarly, if you take an Order Line and look at the Line Items for the associated Order, you should see the original Order Line in the collection. This property holds true within all three perspectives.

There are several ways of naming associations. Traditional data modelers like to name an association using a verb phrase so that the relationship can be used in a sentence. Most object modelers prefer to use nouns to name one or the other of the roles, since that corresponds better to responsibilities and operations.

Some people name every association. I choose to name an association only when doing so improves understanding. I've seen too many associations with names like "has" or "is related to." If there is no name on the role, I consider the name of the role to be the name of the target class, as I indicated previously.

Attributes

Attributes are very similar to associations.

At the conceptual level, a Customer's name attribute indicates that Customers have names. At the specification level, this attribute indicates that a Customer object can tell you its name and has some way of setting a name. At the implementation level, a Customer has a **field** (also called an instance variable or a data member) for its name.

Depending on the detail in the diagram, the notation for an attribute can show the attribute's name, type, and default value (the UML syntax is *visibility name: type = defaultValue*, where *visibility* is the same as for operations, described in the next section).

So what is the difference between an attribute and an association?

From the conceptual perspective, there is no difference—an attribute carries just another kind of notation that you can use if it seems convenient. Attributes are always single-valued. Usually, a diagram doesn't indicate whether an attribute is optional or mandatory (although strictly speaking, it should).

The difference occurs at the specification and implementation levels. Attributes imply navigability from the type to the attribute only. Furthermore, it is implied that the type contains solely its own copy of the attribute object, implying that any type used as an attribute has value rather than reference semantics.

I'll talk about value and reference types later on. For the moment, it's best to think of attributes as small, simple classes, such as strings, dates, money objects, and non-object values, such as *int* and *real*.

Operations

Operations are the processes that a class knows to carry out. They most obviously correspond to the methods on a class. At the specification level, operations correspond to public methods on a type. Normally, you don't show those operations that simply manipulate attributes, because they can usually be inferred. You may need to indicate, however, whether a given attribute is read-only or **immutable** (that is, its value never changes). In the implementation model, you may want to show private and protected operations, as well.

The full UML syntax for operations is

visibility name (parameter-list) : return-type-expression {property-string}

where

- *visibility* is + (public), # (protected), or − (private)
- *name* is a string
- *parameter-list* contains (optional) arguments whose syntax is the same as that for attributes
- *return-type-expression* is an optional, language-dependent specification
- *property-string* indicates property values that apply to the given operation

An example operation might be: + *latestAmountOf (PhenomenonType value) : Quantity*

Within conceptual models, operations should not attempt to specify the interface of a class. Instead, they should indicate the principal responsibilities of that class, perhaps using a couple of words summarizing a CRC responsibility (see sidebar).

CRC Cards

In the late 1980s, one the biggest centers of object technology was the research labs of Tektronix, in Portland, Oregon. These labs had some of the main users of Smalltalk, and many key ideas in object technology were developed there. Two renowned Smalltalk programmers there were Ward Cunningham and Kent Beck.

Cunningham and Beck were and are concerned about how to teach the deep knowledge of Smalltalk they had gained. From this question of how to teach objects came the simple technique of Class-Responsibility-Collaboration (CRC) Cards.

Rather than use diagrams to develop models, as most methodologists did, Cunningham and Beck represented classes on 4 x 6 index cards. And rather than indicate attributes and methods on the cards, they wrote responsibilities.

So what is a responsibility? It is really a high-level description of the purpose of the class. The idea is to try to get away from a description of bits of data and process and instead capture the purpose of the class in a few sentences. The choice of a card is deliberate. You are not allowed to write more than will fit on the card (see Figure 4-4).

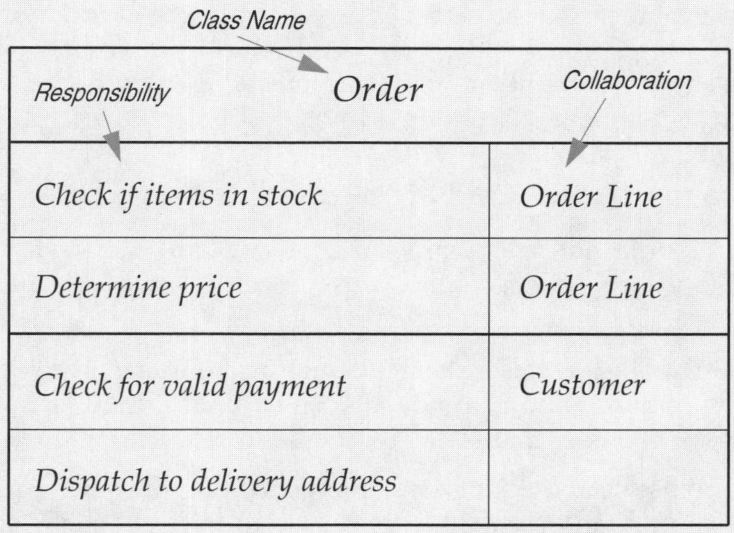

Class Name	
Responsibility *Order*	*Collaboration*
Check if items in stock	Order Line
Determine price	Order Line
Check for valid payment	Customer
Dispatch to delivery address	

Figure 4-4: *Class-Responsibility-Collaboration (CRC) Card*

The second C refers to collaborators. With each responsibility, you indicate which other classes you need to work with to fulfill it. This gives you some idea of the links between classes—still at a high level.

One of the chief benefits of CRC cards is that they encourage animated discussion among the developers. They are especially effective when you are walking through a use case to see how the classes are going to implement it. Developers pick cards as each class collaborates in the use case. As ideas about responsibilities are formed, you can write them on the cards. Thinking about responsibilities is important, because it gets you away from classes as dumb data holders and eases the team members toward understanding the higher-level behavior of each class.

A common mistake I see people make is generating long lists of low-level responsibilities. This is really missing the point. The responsibilities should easily fit on a card. I would question any card with more than three responsibilities. Ask yourself if the class should be split or if the responsibilities would be better stated by rolling them up into higher-level statements.

When to Use CRC Cards

Some people find CRC cards to be wonderful; others find the technique leaves them cold.

I certainly think you should try them out to see if the team likes working with them. Use them especially if your teams are getting bogged down in too many details too early or if they seem to be identifying classes that seem cluttered and lack clear definitions.

You can use class diagrams and interaction diagrams (see Chapter 6) to capture and formalize the results of CRC modeling into a UML-notated design. Ensure that each class within your class diagrams has a statement of its responsibilities.

Where to Find Out More

Sadly, Cunningham and Beck have never written a book about CRC, but you can find their original paper (Beck and Cunningham 1989) on the Web (<**http://c2.com/doc/oopsla89/paper.html**>). On the whole, the book that best describes this technique and, indeed, the whole notion of using responsibilities, is Rebecca Wirfs-Brock's (1990). It is a relatively old book by OO standards, but it has aged well.

I often find it useful to distinguish between operations that change the state of a class and those that don't. A **query** is an operation that gets a value from a class without changing that class' observable state. The **observable state** of an object is the state you can determine from its associated queries.

Consider an Account object that calculates its balance from a list of entries. To improve performance, Account might cache the result of the balance calculation in a field for future queries. So if the cache is empty, the first time the "balance" operation is called, it puts the result into the cache field. The "balance" operation thus changes the actual state of the Account object but not the observable state because all queries return the same value whether or not the cache is full. Operations that do change the observable state of an object are called **modifiers.**

I find it helpful to be clear about the difference between queries and modifiers. Queries can be executed in any order, but the sequence of modifiers is more important. It's my practice to avoid returning values from modifiers in order to keep them separate.

Other terms you sometimes see are getting methods and setting methods. A **getting method** is a method that returns a value from a field (and does nothing else). A **setting method** puts a value into a field (and does nothing else). From the outside, a client should not be able to tell if a query is a getting method nor if a modifier is a setting method. Knowledge of getting and setting methods is entirely internal to the class.

Another distinction is between operation and method. An **operation** is something that is invoked on an object (the procedure call) while a **method** is the body of procedure. The two are different when you have polymorphism. If you have a supertype with three subtypes, each of which overrides the supertype's "foo" operation, you have one operation and four methods that implement it.

People usually use operation and method interchangeably, but there are times when it is useful to be precise about the difference. Sometimes, people distinguish them by using the terms method call or method declaration (for operation) and method body.

Languages have their own naming conventions. In C++, operations are called member functions, while Smalltalk calls operations methods. C++ also uses the term members of a class to mean a class's operations and methods.

Generalization

A typical example of **generalization** involves the personal and corporate customers of a business. They have differences but also many similarities. The similarities can be placed in a general Customer class (the supertype) with Personal Customer and Corporate Customer as subtypes.

This phenomenon is also subject to different interpretations at the different levels of modeling. Conceptually, for instance, we can say that Corporate Customer is a subtype of Customer if all instances of Corporate Customer are also, by definition, instances of Customer. A Corporate Customer is then a special kind of Customer. The key idea is that everything we say about a Customer (associations, attributes, operations) is true also for a Corporate Customer.

Within a specification model, generalization means that the interface of the subtype must include all elements from the interface of the supertype. The subtype's interface is said to **conform to** the supertype's interface.

Another way of thinking of this involves the principle of **substitutability**. I should be able to substitute a Corporate Customer within any code that requires a Customer, and everything should work fine. Essentially, this means that if I write code assuming I have a Customer, then I can freely use any subtype of Customer. The Corporate Customer may respond to certain commands differently from another Customer (per the principle of polymorphism), but the caller should not need to worry about the difference.

Generalization at the implementation perspective is associated with inheritance in programming languages. The subclass inherits all the methods and fields of the superclass and may override inherited methods.

The key point here is the difference between generalization at the specification perspective (subtyping, or interface-inheritance) and at the implementation perspective (subclassing, or implementation-inheritance). Subclassing is one way to implement subtyping. You can also implement subtyping through delegation—indeed, many of the patterns described in Gamma *et al.* (1994) are about ways of having two classes with similar interfaces without using subclassing. You might also look at Martin and Odell's "pragmatics" book (1996) or Fowler (1997) for other ideas on implementations for subtyping.

With either of these forms of generalization, you should always ensure that the conceptual generalization also applies. I have found that if you don't do this, you run into trouble because the generalization is not stable when you make changes later on.

Sometimes, you come across cases in which a subtype has the same interface as its supertype but the subtype implements operations in a different way. If you do, you may choose not to show the subtype on a specification-perspective diagram. I usually do if the users of the class would find it of interest that types may exist, but I don't if the subtypes are varied only because of internal implementation reasons.

Constraint Rules

Much of what you are doing in drawing a class diagram is indicating constraints.

Figure 4-3 indicates that an Order can be placed only by a single Customer. The diagram also implies that each Line Item is thought of separately: You say 40 brown widgets, 40 blue widgets, and 40 red widgets, not 40 red, blue, and brown widgets. Further, the diagram says that Corporate Customers have credit limits but Personal Customers do not.

The basic constructs of association, attribute, and generalization do much to specify important constraints, but they cannot indicate every constraint. These constraints still need to be captured; the class diagram is a good place to do that.

The UML defines no strict syntax for describing constraints other than putting them inside braces ({}). I like using an informal English, emphasizing readability. You can also use a more formal statement, such as predicate calculus or some derivative. Another option is to use a fragment of program code.

Ideally, rules should be implemented as assertions in your programming language. These correspond with the Design by Contract notion of invariants (see sidebar). I like to create a *checkInvariant* method on classes that have invariants and call it within debug code to help check invariants.

Design by Contract

Design by Contract is a design technique developed by Bertrand Meyer. The technique is a central feature of the Eiffel language that he developed. Design by Contract is not specific to Eiffel, however; it is a valuable technique that can be used with any programming language.

At the heart of Design by Contract is the assertion. An **assertion** is a Boolean statement that should never be false and, therefore, will only be false because of a bug. Typically, assertions are checked only during debug and are not checked during production execution. Indeed, a program should never assume that assertions are being checked.

Design by Contract uses three kinds of assertions: post-conditions, pre-conditions, and invariants.

Pre-conditions and post-conditions apply to operations. A **post-condition** is a statement of what the world should look like after execution of an operation. For instance, if we define the operation "square" on a number, the post-condition would take the form *result = this * this*, where *result* is the output and *this* is the object on which the operation was invoked. The post-condition is a useful way of saying what we do without saying how we do it—in other words, of separating interface from implementation.

A **pre-condition** is a statement of how we expect the world to be before we execute an operation. We might define a pre-condition for the "square" operation of *this >= 0*. Such a pre-condition says that it is an error to invoke "square" on a negative number and that the consequences of doing so are undefined.

On first glance, this seems a bad idea, because we should put some check somewhere to ensure that "square" is invoked properly. The important question is who is responsible for doing so.

The pre-condition makes it explicit that the caller is responsible for checking. Without this explicit statement of responsibilities, we can get either too little checking (because both parties assume that the other is responsible) or too much (both parties check). Too much checking is a bad thing, because it leads to lots of duplicate checking code, which can significantly increase the complexity of a program. Being explicit about who is responsible helps to reduce this complexity. The danger that the caller forgets to check is reduced by the fact that assertions are usually checked during debugging and testing.

From these definitions of pre-condition and post-condition, we can see a strong definition of the term **exception**, which occurs when an operation is invoked with its pre-condition satisfied, yet it cannot return with its post-condition satisfied.

An **invariant** is an assertion about a class. For instance, an Account class may have an invariant that says that *balance == sum(entries.amount())*. The invariant is "always" true for all instances of the class. Here, "always" means "whenever the object is available to have an operation invoked on it."

In essence, this means that the invariant is added to pre-conditions and post-conditions associated with all public operations of the given class. The invariant may become false during execution of a method, but it should be restored to true by the time any other object can do anything to the receiver.

Assertions can play a unique role in subclassing.

One of the dangers of polymorphism is that you could redefine a subclass's operations to be inconsistent with the superclass's operations. Assertions stop you from doing this. The invariants and post-conditions of a class must apply to all subclasses. The subclasses can choose to strengthen these assertions, but they cannot weaken them. The pre-condition, on the other hand, cannot be strengthened but may be weakened.

This looks odd at first, but it is important to allow dynamic binding. You should always be able to treat a subclass object as if it were an instance of the superclass (per the principle of substitutability). If a subclass strengthened its pre-condition, then a superclass operation could fail when applied to the subclass.

Essentially, assertions can only increase the responsibilities of the subclass. Pre-conditions are a statement of passing a responsibility on to the caller; you increase the responsibilities of a class by weakening a pre-condition. In practice, all of this allows much better control of subclassing and helps you to ensure that subclasses behave properly.

Ideally, assertions should be included in the code as part of the interface definition. Compilers should be able to turn assertion checking on for debugging and remove it for production use. Various stages of assertion checking can be used. Pre-conditions often give you the best chances of catching errors for the least amount of processing overhead.

When to Use Design by Contract

Design by Contract is a valuable technique that you should use whenever you program. It is particular helpful in building clear interfaces.

Only Eiffel supports assertions as part of its language, but Eiffel is, unfortunately, not a widely used language. It is straightforward to add mechanisms to C++ and Smalltalk to support some assertions. It is rather more awkward to do so to Java, but it is possible.

UML does not talk much about assertions, but you can use them without any trouble. Invariants are equivalent to constraint rules on class diagrams, and you should use these as much as possible. Operation pre-conditions and post-conditions should be documented within your operation definitions.

Where to Find Out More

Meyer's book (1997) is a classic (albeit now huge) work on OO design that talks a lot about assertions. Kim Walden and Jean-Marc Nerson (1995) and Steve Cook and John Daniels (1994) use Design by Contract extensively in their books.

You can also get more information from ISE (Bertrand Meyer's company) at <**www.eiffel.com**>.

When to Use Class Diagrams

Class diagrams are the backbone of nearly all OO methods, so you will find yourself using them all the time. This chapter covers the basic concepts; Chapter 5 discusses many of the advanced concepts.

The trouble with class diagrams is that they are so rich that they can be overwhelming to use. Here are a few tips.

- Don't try to use all the notations available to you. Start with the simple stuff in this chapter: classes, associations, attributes, and generalization. Introduce other notations from Chapter 5 only when you need them.

- Fit the perspective from which you are drawing the models to the stage of the project.
  - — If you are in analysis, draw conceptual models.
  - — When working with software, concentrate on specification models.
  - — Draw implementation models only when you are illustrating a particular implementation technique.
- Don't draw models for everything; instead, concentrate on the key areas. It is better to have a few diagrams that you use and keep up-to-date than to have many forgotten, obsolete models.

The biggest danger with class diagrams is that you can get bogged down in implementation details far too early. To combat this, focus on the conceptual and specification perspectives. If you run into these problems, you may well find CRC cards (see page 64) to be extremely useful.

Where to Find Out More

The three amigos' books will serve as the definitive reference for class diagrams. My advice about others depends on whether you prefer an implementation or a conceptual perspective. For implementation, try Booch (1994); for a conceptual perspective, try Martin and Odell's "foundations" book (1994). Once you have read your first choice, read the other one—both perspectives are important. After that, any good OO book will add some interesting insights. I particularly like Cook and Daniels (1994) for its treatment of perspectives and the formality that the authors introduce.

Chapter 5

Class Diagrams: Advanced Concepts

The concepts described in Chapter 4 correspond with the key notations in class diagrams. Those are the first ones to understand and become familiar with, as they will comprise 90% of your effort in building class diagrams.

The class diagram technique, however, has bred dozens of notations for additional concepts. I find that I don't use these often, but they are handy when they are appropriate. I'll discuss them one at a time, and point out some of the issues in using them. Remember, however, that they are all optional, and many people have gotten a lot of value out of class diagrams without using these additional items.

You will probably find this chapter somewhat heavy going. The good news is that you can safely skip this chapter during your first pass through the book and come back to it later.

Stereotypes

The idea of **stereotypes** was coined by Rebecca Wirfs-Brock (Wirfs-Brock *et al.* 1990). The concept has been seized with great enthusiasm by the inventors of the UML, albeit in a way that doesn't really mean the same thing. Both ideas have value, however.

The original idea of a stereotype was a high-level classification of an object that gave you some indication of the kind of object it was. An example is the distinction between a "controller" and a "coordinator."

Often, you run into OO designs in which one class seems to do all the work, often via a big *doIt* method, and the other classes basically do nothing but encapsulate data. This is a poor design because it means that the controller is very complex and difficult to deal with.

To improve this, you move behavior from the controller to the relatively dumb data objects, so those objects become more intelligent and get higher-level responsibilities. The controller now becomes a coordinator. The coordinator is responsible for firing off tasks in a particular sequence, but other objects know how to carry out these tasks.

The essence of the stereotype is that it suggests certain outline responsibilities for a class. The UML has taken this idea and turned it into a general extension mechanism for the language itself.

In Jacobson's original work (1994), he classifies all the classes in a system into three classifications: interface objects, control objects, and entity objects. (His control objects are, when well-designed, like Wirfs-Brock's coordinators.) Jacobson suggested rules for how these kinds of classes should communicate and gave each kind a different icon. This distinction is not a core part of the UML. Instead, these kinds of classes are actually stereotypes of classes—indeed, they are very much stereotypes in the Wirfs-Brock sense of the term.

Stereotypes are usually shown in text between guillemots («control object»), but they can also be shown by defining an icon for the stereotype. The idea is that if you are not using Jacobson's approach, you can forget about the stereotypes. If you want to use that approach, you can define the stereotypes and the rules for using them.

Many extensions to the core UML can be described as a collection of stereotypes. Within class diagrams, these might be stereotypes of classes, associations, or generalizations. You can think of the stereotypes as subtypes of the meta-model types Class, Association, and Generalization.

I've noticed that people using the UML tend to get confused between constraints and stereotypes. If you mark a class as abstract, is that a constraint or a stereotype? The current official documents call it a constraint, but you should be aware that there is a blurred usage between the two. This is not surprising as subtypes are often more constrained than supertypes.

Multiple and Dynamic Classification

Classification refers to the relationship between an object and its type.

Most methods make certain assumptions about this type of relationship—assumptions that are also present in mainstream OO programming languages. These assumptions were questioned by Jim Odell, who felt that they were too restrictive for conceptual modeling. The assumptions are of single, static classification of objects; Odell suggests using multiple, dynamic classification of objects for conceptual models.

In **single classification**, an object belongs to a single type, which may inherit from supertypes. In **multiple classification**, an object may be described by several types that are not necessarily connected by inheritance.

Note that multiple classification is different from multiple inheritance. Multiple inheritance says a type may have many supertypes, but that a single type must be defined for each object. Multiple classification allows multiple types for an object without defining a specific type for the purpose.

As an example of this, consider a person subtyped as either man or woman, doctor or nurse, patient or not (see Figure 5-1). Multiple classification allows an object to have any of these types assigned to it in any allowable combination without the need for types to be defined for all the legal combinations.

If you use multiple classification, you need to be sure that you make it clear which combinations are legal. You do this by labeling a generalization line with a **discriminator**, which is an indication of the basis of the subtyping. Several subtypes can share the same discriminator. All subtypes with the same discriminator are disjoint—that is, any instance of the supertype may be an instance of only one of the subtypes within that discriminator. A good convention is to have all subclasses that use one discriminator roll up to one triangle, as shown in Figure 5-1. Alternatively, you can have several arrows with the same text label.

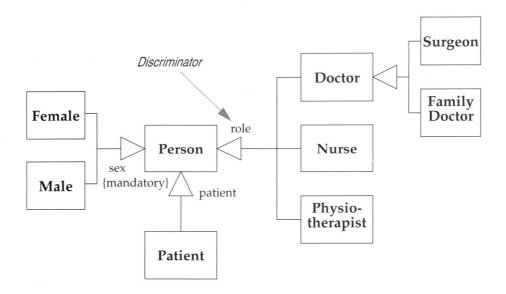

Figure 5-1: *Multiple Classification*

A useful (but non standard UML) constraint is to mark the discriminator as {mandatory}. This means that any instance of the superclass must be an instance of one of the subclasses in that group. (The superclass is then abstract.)

To illustrate, note the following legal combinations of subtypes in the diagram: (Female, Patient, Nurse); (Male, Physiotherapist); (Female, Patient); and (Female, Doctor, Surgeon). Note also that combinations such as (Patient, Doctor) and (Male, Doctor, Nurse) are illegal: The former because it doesn't include a type from the {mandatory} Sex discriminator; the latter because it contains two types from the Role discriminator. Single classification, by definition, corresponds to a single, unlabeled discriminator.

Another question is whether an object may change its type. A good example here is of a bank account. When the account is overdrawn, it substantially changes its behavior—specifically, several operations (including "withdraw" and "close") get overridden.

Dynamic classification allows objects to change type within the subtyping structure; **static classification** does not. With static classification, a separation is made between types and states; dynamic classification combines these notions.

Should you use multiple, dynamic classification? I believe it is useful for conceptual modeling. You can do it with specification modeling, but you have to be comfortable with the techniques for implementing it. The trick is to implement in such a way that it looks the same as subclassing from the interface so that a user of a class cannot tell which implementation is being used. (See Fowler 1997 for some techniques.) However, like most of these things, the choice depends on the circumstances, and you have to use your best judgment. The transformation from a multiple, dynamic interface to a single static implementation may well be more trouble than it is worth.

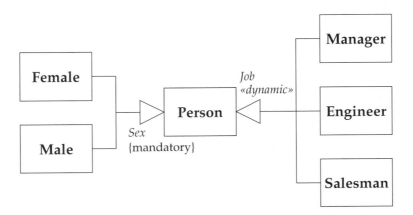

Figure 5-2: *Dynamic Classification*

Figure 5-2 shows an example of using dynamic classification for a person's job, which, of course, can change. This can be appropriate, but the subtypes would need additional behavior, instead of being just labels. In these cases, it is often worth creating a separate class for the job and linking the person to it with an association. I wrote a pattern, called *Role Models*, on this subject; you can find information about this pattern, and other information that supplements my *Analysis Patterns* book, at <**http://www.aw.com/cp/fowler.html**>.

Aggregation and Composition

One of my biggest *bêtes noires* in modeling is aggregation. It's easy to explain glibly: **Aggregation** is the part-of relationship. It's like saying a car has an engine and wheels as its parts. This sounds good, but the difficult thing is considering what the difference is between aggregation and association.

Peter Coad gave an example of aggregation as the relationship between an organization and its clerks; Jim Rumbaugh stated that a company is not an aggregation of its employees. When the gurus can't agree, what are we to do? The trouble is, there is no single accepted definition of the difference between aggregation and association used by all methodologists.

In fact, few of them use any kind of formal definition. The important practical thing is that everyone employs a slightly different notion, so you have to beware of the concept. I have always been wary of the concept, and I usually prefer to avoid it unless the project team agrees on some rigorous and useful meaning.

In addition to plain aggregation, the UML offers a stronger variety of aggregation, called composition. With **composition**, the part object may belong to only one whole; further, the parts are usually expected to live and die with the whole. Any deletion of the whole is considered to cascade to the parts.

This cascading delete is often considered to be a defining part of aggregation, but it is implied by any role with a 1..1 multiplicity; if you really want to delete a Customer, for instance, you must cascade that delete to Orders (and thus to Order Lines).

Figure 5-3 shows examples of these constructs. The compositions to *Point* indicate that any instance of *Point* may be in either a *Polygon* or a *Circle*, but not both. An instance of *Style*, however, may be shared by many *Polygons* and *Circles*. Furthermore, this implies that deleting a *Polygon* would cause its associated *Points* to be deleted, but **not** the associated *Style*.

This constraint—that a *Point* may appear in only one *Polygon* or *Circle* at a time—could not be expressed by the multiplicities alone. It also implies that the point is a value object (see page 88). You can add a multiplicity to a composite side of the association, but I don't bother. The black diamond says all that needs to be said.

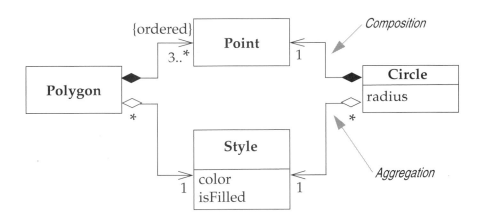

Figure 5-3: *Aggregation and Composition*

Figure 5-4 shows another notation for composition. In this case, you put the component inside the whole. The component class's name is not bold, and you write it in the form *rolename:Class name*. In addition, you put the multiplicity in the top right corner.

Different composition notations work for different situations. There are a couple more, although the variety of composition notations offered by the UML does get rather overwhelming. Note that these variations can be used only for composition, not aggregation.

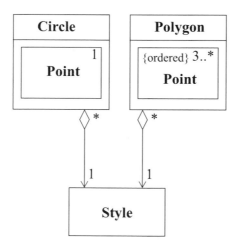

Figure 5-4: *Alternative Notation for Composition*

Derived Associations and Attributes

Derived associations and **derived attributes** are those that can be calculated from other associations and attributes, respectively, on a class diagram. For example, an age attribute of a Person can be derived if you know that Person's date of birth.

Each perspective brings its own interpretation of derived features on class diagrams. The most critical of these has to do with the specification perspective. From this angle, it is important to realize that derived features indicate a constraint between values, not a statement of what is calculated and what is stored.

Figure 5-5 shows a hierarchical structure of accounts drawn from a specification perspective. The model uses the *Composite* pattern (see Gamma *et al.* 1994).

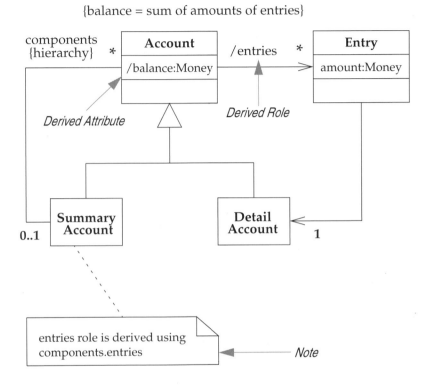

Figure 5-5: *Derived Associations and Attributes*

Note the following.

- Entry objects are attached to Detail Accounts.
- The balance of an Account is calculated as the sum of Entry amounts.
- A Summary Account's entries are the entries of its components, determined recursively.

Since Figure 5-5 illustrates a specification model, it does not state that Accounts do not contain fields to hold balances; such a cache may well be present, but it is hidden from the clients of the Account class.

Figure 5-6: *Time Period Class*

I can illustrate how derived elements indicate constraints with a class named Time Period (see Figure 5-6).

If this is a specification diagram, then although it suggests that *start* and *end* are stored and *duration* is calculated, a programmer can, in fact, implement this class in any fashion that maintains that external behavior. For instance, storing *start* and *duration* and calculating *end* is perfectly acceptable.

On implementation diagrams, derived values are valuable for annotating fields that are used as caches for performance reasons. By marking them and recording the derivation of the cache, it is easier to see explicitly what the cache is doing. I often reinforce this in the code by using the word "cache" on such a field (for instance, *balanceCache*).

On conceptual diagrams, I use derived markers to remind me where these derivations exist and to confirm with the domain experts that the derivations exist. They then correlate with their use in specification diagrams.

In the worlds of OMT and Odell, you showed a derived association by a slash on the association line. This usage is not part of the UML, but I confess I do it anyway—it looks clearer, particularly when I don't name the association.

Interfaces and Abstract Classes

One of the great qualities of object-oriented development is that you can vary the interfaces of classes independent of the implementation. Much of the power of object development comes from this property. However, few people make good use of it.

Programming languages use a single construct, the class, which contains both interface and implementation. When you subclass, you inherit both. Using the interface as a separate construct is rarely used, which is a shame.

A pure interface (as in Java) is a class with no implementation, and, therefore, has operation declarations but no method bodies and no fields. Interfaces are often declared through abstract classes. Such classes may provide some implementation, but often they are used primarily to declare an interface. The point is that subclassing (or some other mechanism) will provide the implementation, but clients will never see the implementation, only the interface.

The text editor represented in Figure 5-7 is a typical example of this. To allow the editor to be platform-independent, we define a platform-independent abstract Window class. This class has no operations; it only defines an interface for the text editor to use. Platform-specific subclasses can be used as desired.

If you have an abstract class or method, the UML convention is to italicize the name of the abstract item. You can use the {abstract} constraint, as well (or instead). I use {abstract} on whiteboards because I can't write italic text. With a diagramming tool, however, I prefer the elegance of italics.

Subclassing is not the only way to do this, however. Java provides a specific interface, and the compiler checks that the class provides an implementation for all operations defined for that interface.

In Figure 5-8, we see InputStream, DataInput, and DataInputStream (defined in the standard *java.io* file). InputStream is an abstract class; DataInput is an interface.

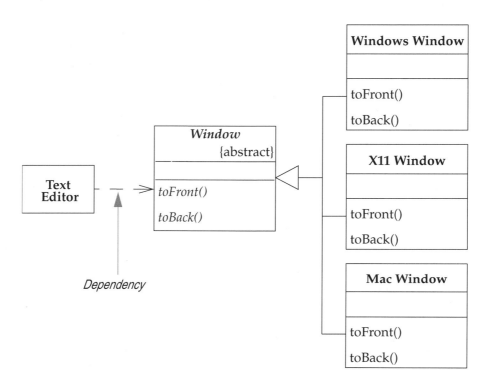

Figure 5-7: *Window as Abstract Class*

Some client class, say, OrderReader, needs to use DataInput's functionality. The DataInputStream class implements both the DataInput and InputStream interfaces and is a subclass of the latter.

The link between DataInputStream and DataInput is a refinement relationship. **Refinement** is a general term used in the UML to indicate a greater level of detail. It can be used for implementation of interfaces or for some other purposes (see the three amigos' books for specifics). Refinement is deliberately similar to generalization.

In a specification model, both subclassing and refinement would be represented as subtyping; the distinction between refinement and generalization is valid only for implementation models. Some modelers would prefer to use «type» rather than «interface». I prefer «interface» because it makes the role of the interface explicit.

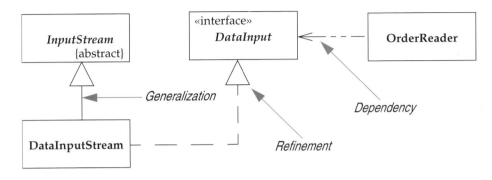

Figure 5-8: *Interfaces and Abstract Class: An Example from Java*

The link between OrderReader and DataInput is a dependency. It shows that the OrderReader uses the DataInput interface for some purpose. I will talk more about dependencies in Chapter 7. Essentially, a dependency indicates that if the DataInput interface changes, the OrderReader may also have to change. One of the aims of development is to keep dependencies to a minimum so that the effects of changes are minimized.

Figure 5-9 shows an alternative, more compact notation. Here, the interfaces are represented by small circles (often called lollipops) coming off the classes that implement them.

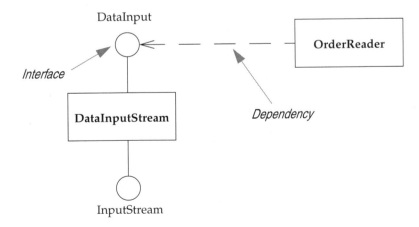

Figure 5-9: *Lollipop Notation for Interfaces*

There is no distinction between refining an interface and subclassing an abstract class.

Abstract classes and interfaces are similar, but there is a difference. Both allow you to define an interface and defer its implementation until later. However, the abstract class allows you to add implementation of some of the methods; an interface forces you to defer definition of all methods.

Reference Objects and Value Objects

One of the common things said about objects is that they have identity. This is true, but it is not quite as simple as that. In practice, you find that identity is important for reference objects, but not so important for value objects.

Reference objects are things like Customer. Here, identity is very important, because you usually want only one software object to designate a customer in the real world. Any object that references a Customer object will do so through a reference or pointer; all objects that reference this Customer will reference the same software object. That way, changes to a Customer are available to all users of the Customer.

If you have two references to a Customer and you wish to see if they are the same, you usually compare their identities. Copies may be disallowed, and if they are allowed, they tend to be made rarely, perhaps for archive purposes or for replication across a network. If copies are made, you need to sort out how to synchronize changes.

Value objects are things like Date. You often have multiple value objects representing the same object in the real world. For example, it is normal to have hundreds of objects that designate 1–Jan–97. These are all interchangeable copies. New dates are created and destroyed frequently.

If you have two dates and wish to see if they are the same, you don't look at their identities—you look at the values they represent. This usually means you have to write an equality test operator, which for dates would make a test on year, month, and day (or whatever the internal representation is). Usually each object that references 1–Jan–97 has its own dedicated object, but sometimes you do get shared dates.

Value objects should be **immutable**. In other words, you should not be able to take a date object of 1–Jan–97 and change the same date object to be 2–Jan–97. Instead, you should create a new 2–Jan–97 object and link to that first object. The reason for this is that if the date were shared, you would update another object's date in an unpredictable way.

In C++, this is not an issue because you try hard not to share dates; sharing value objects leads to memory management problems. In place of that, you can override assignment to make copies. Within memory-managed environments such as Java, this is more important, especially since dates are not immutable in Java. As a rule of thumb, don't change a value object.

In days gone by, the difference between reference objects and value objects was clearer. Value objects were the built-in values of the type system. Now you can extend the type system with your own classes, so this issue requires more thought. Within the UML, attributes are usually used for value objects and associations are used for reference objects. You can also use composition for value objects.

I don't find that the distinction between reference and value objects is useful with conceptual models. There is no difference between the two constructs from the conceptual perspective. If I represent a link to a value object with an association, I usually mark the multiplicity of the role from the value to its user as *, unless there is a uniqueness rule (such as a sequence number).

Collections for Multi-Valued Roles

A **multi-valued role** is one whose multiplicity's upper bound is greater than 1 (for instance, *). The usual convention is that multi-valued roles are thought of as sets. There is no ordering for the target objects, and no target object appears in the role more than once. You can change these assumptions, however, by attaching a constraint.

The *{ordered}* constraint implies that there is an ordering to the target objects (that is, the target objects form a list). Target objects may appear only once in the list.

I use the *{bag}* constraint to indicate that target objects may appear more than once, but there is no ordering. (If I want ordering and multiple appearances, I would use *{ordered bag}*, although I haven't needed to do that yet.) I also use the *{hierarchy}* constraint to indicate that the target objects form a hierarchy, and I use the *{dag}* constraint to indicate a directed acyclic graph.

Frozen

Frozen is a constraint that the UML defines as applicable to a role, but which can usefully be applied to attributes and classes as well.

On an attribute or role, frozen indicates that the value of that attribute or role may not change during the lifetime of the source object. The value must be set at object creation and may never change after that. The initial value may be null. Of course, if that's true when the object is constructed, it will be true as long as the object is alive. This implies that there must be an argument for this value in a constructor, and that there is no command operation that updates this value.

When applied to a class, frozen indicates that all roles and attributes associated with that class are frozen.

Frozen is *not* the same as read-only. Read-only implies that a value cannot be changed directly but may change due to a change in some other value. For instance, if a person has a date of birth and an age, then the age may be read-only, but it cannot be frozen. I mark "freezing" using the *{frozen}* constraint, and I mark read-only values with *{read only}*.

If you are thinking of "freezing" something, bear in mind that people make mistakes. In software, we model what we know about the world, not how the world is. If we were modeling how the world is, a "date of birth" attribute for a Person object would be frozen, but for most cases, we would want to change it if we found that a previous recording was incorrect.

Classification and Generalization

I often hear people talk about subtyping as the "is a" relationship. I urge you to beware of that way of thinking. The problem is that the phrase "is a" can mean different things.

Consider the following phrases.

1. Shep is a Border Collie.
2. A Border Collie is a Dog.
3. Dogs are Animals.
4. A Border Collie is a Breed.
5. Dog is a Species.

Now try combining the phrases. If I combine phrases 1 and 2, I get "Shep is a Dog"; 2 and 3 taken together yield "Border Collies are Animals." And 1 plus 2 plus 3 gives me "Shep is an Animal." So far, so good. Now try 1 and 4: "Shep is a Breed." The combination of 2 and 5 is "A Border Collie is a Species." These are not so good.

Why can I combine some of these phrases and not others? The reason is that some are **classification** (the object Shep is an instance of the type Border Collie) and some are **generalization** (the type Border Collie is a subtype of the type Dog). Generalization is transitive, classification is not. I can combine a classification followed by a generalization, but not vice versa.

I make this point to get you to be wary of "is a." Using it can lead to inappropriate use of subclassing and confused responsibilities. Better tests for subtyping in this case would be the phrases "Dogs are kinds of Animals" and "Every instance of a Border Collie is an instance of a Dog."

Qualified Associations

A **qualified association** is the UML equivalent of a programming concept variously known as associative arrays, maps, and dictionaries.

Figure 5-10: *Qualified Association*

Figure 5-10 shows a way of representing the association between the Order and Order Line classes that uses a qualifier. The qualifier says that in connection with an Order, there may be one Order Line for each instance of Product.

Conceptually, this example indicates that you cannot have two Order Lines within an Order for the same Product. From a specification perspective, this qualified association would imply an interface along the lines of

```
class Order {

    public OrderLine lineItem (Product aProduct);

    public void addLineItem (Number amount,
        Product forProduct);
```

Thus, all access to a given Line Item requires the identity of a Product as an argument. A multiplicity of 1 would indicate that there must be a Line Item for every Product; * would indicate that you can have multiple Order Lines per Product but that access to the Line Items is still indexed by Product.

From an implementation perspective, this suggests the use of an associative array or similar data structure to hold the order lines.

```
Class Order {

    private Dictionary _lineItems;
```

In conceptual modeling, I use the qualifier construct only to show constraints along the lines of "single Order Line per Product on Order." In specification models, I use it to show a keyed lookup interface. I'm quite happy to use both this and an unqualified association at the same time if that is a suitable interface.

I use qualifiers within implementation models to show uses of an associative array or similar data structure. (See the discussion of the *Keyed Mapping* pattern in Fowler 1997 for more information about my use of qualifiers.)

Association Class

Association classes allow you to add attributes, operations, and other features to associations, as shown in Figure 5-11.

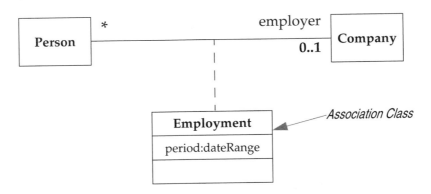

Figure 5-11: *Association Class*

We can see from the diagram that a Person may work for a single Company. We need to keep information about the period of time that each employee works for each Company.

We can do this by adding a *dateRange* attribute to the association. We could add this attribute to the Person class, but it is really a fact about a Person's relationship to a Company, which will change should the person's employer change.

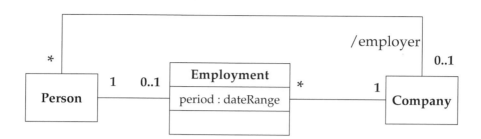

Figure 5-12: *Promoting an Association Class to a Full Class*

Figure 5-12 shows another way to represent this information: make Employment a full class in its own right. (Note how the multiplicities have been moved accordingly.) In this case, each of the classes in the original association has a single-valued role with regard to the Employment class. The "employer" role now is derived, although you don't have to show this.

What benefit do you gain with the association class to offset the extra notation you have to remember? The association class adds an extra constraint, in that there can be only one instance of the association class between any two participating objects. I feel the need for an example.

Take a look at the two diagrams contained in Figure 5-13. These diagrams have much the same form. However, we could imagine a Person working for the same Company at different periods of time (that is, he or she leaves and later returns). This means that a Person could have more than one Employment association with the same Company over time. With regard to the Person and Skill classes, it would be hard to see why a Person would have more than one Competency in the same Skill—indeed, you would probably consider that an error.

In the UML, only the latter case is legal. You can have only one Competency for each combination of Person and Skill. The top diagram in Figure 5-13 would not allow a Person to have more than one Employment with the same Company. If you need to allow this, you need to make Employment a full class, in the style of Figure 5-12.

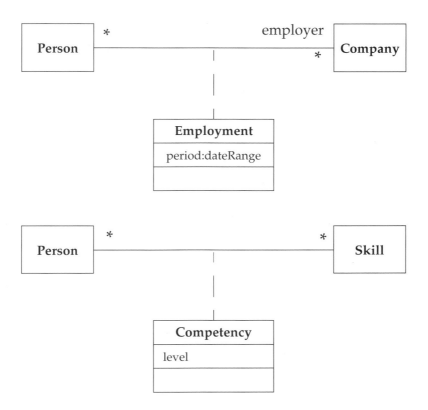

Figure 5-13: *Association Class Subtleties*

In the past, modelers made various assumptions about the meaning of an association class in these circumstances. Some assumed that you can have only unique combinations (such as competency), while others did not assume such a constraint. Many people did not think about it at all and may have assumed the constraint in some places and not in others. So when using the UML, remember that the constraint is always there.

You often find this kind of construct with historic information, such as in the Employment case above. A useful pattern here is the *Historic Mapping* pattern described in Fowler (1997). We can use this by defining a «history» stereotype (see Figure 5-14).

Figure 5-14: *History Stereotype for Associations*

The model indicates that a Person may only work for a single Company at one time. Over time, however, a Person may work for several Companies. This suggests an interface along the lines of

```
class Person {

  //get current employer
  Company employer();

  //employer at a given date
  Company employer(Date);

  void changeEmployer(Company newEmployer,
      Date changeDate);

  void leaveEmployer (Date changeDate);
```

The «history» stereotype is not part of the UML, but I mention it here for two reasons. First, it is a notion I have found useful on several occasions in my modeling career. Second, it shows how you can use stereotypes to extend the UML.

Parameterized Class

Several languages, most noticeably C++, have the notion of a **parameterized class** (also known as a **template**).

This concept is most obviously useful for working with collections in a strongly typed language. This way, you can define behavior for sets in general by defining a template class Set.

```
class Set <T> {
    void insert (T newElement);
    void remove (T anElement);
```

When you have done this, you can use the general definition to make set classes for more specific elements.

```
Set <Employee> employeeSet;
```

You declare a parameterized class in the UML using the notation shown in Figure 5-15.

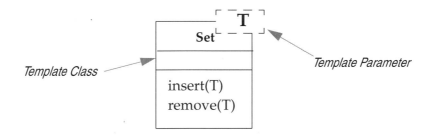

Figure 5-15: *Parameterized Class*

The T in the diagram is a placeholder for the type parameter. (You may have more than one.) In an untyped language, such as Smalltalk, this issue does not come up, so this concept is not useful.

A use of a parameterized class, such as *Set<Employee>* from above, is called a **bound element**.

You can show a bound element in two ways. The first way mirrors the C++ syntax (see Figure 5-16).

Figure 5-16: *Bound Element (Version 1)*

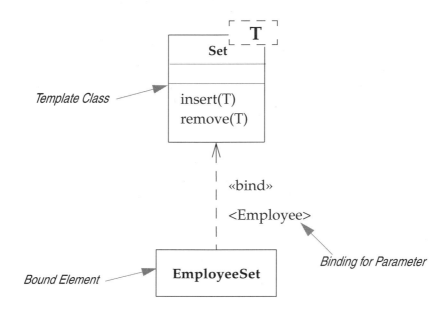

Figure 5-17: *Bound Element (Version 2)*

The alternative notation (see Figure 5-17) reinforces the link to the template and allows you to rename the bound element.

The «bind» stereotype is a stereotype on the refinement relationship. This relationship indicates that EmployeeSet will conform to the interface of Set. In specification terms, the EmployeeSet is a subtype of Set. This fits the other way of implementing type-specific collections, which is to declare all appropriate subtypes.

Using a bound element is *not* the same as subtyping, however. You are not allowed to add features to the bound element: it is completely specified by its template; you are adding only restricting type information. If you want to add features, you must create a subtype.

Although collections are the classic use for parameterized classes, there are many other ways to use them in C++ (see Koenig 1996 for other ideas).

Parameterized classes allow you to use a derived typing. When you write the body of the template, you may invoke operations on the parameter. When you later declare a bound element, the compiler tries to ensure that the supplied parameter supports the operations required by the template.

This is a derived typing mechanism because you do not have to define a type for the parameter; the compiler figures out if the binding is viable by looking at the source of the template. This property is central to the use of parameterized classes in C++'s STL; these classes can also be used for other interesting tricks.

Using parameterized classes does have repercussions—for example, they can cause considerable code bloat in C++. I rarely use parameterized classes in conceptual modeling, mostly because they are used mainly for collections, which are implied by associations. (One case I do use it for is the *Range* pattern; see Fowler 1997). I only use parameterized classes in specification and implementation modeling if they are supported by the language I am using.

Visibility

I must confess to having some trepidation about this section.

Visibility is one of those subjects that is simple in principle but has complex subtleties. The simple idea is that any class has public and private elements. Public elements can be used by any other class; private elements can be used only by the owning class. However, each language makes its own rules. Although they all use terms such as "public," "private," and "protected," these terms mean different things in different languages. These differences are small, but they lead to confusion, especially for those of us who use more than one language.

The UML tries to address this without getting into a horrible tangle. Essentially, within the UML, you can tag any attribute or operation with a visibility indicator. You can use any marker you like, and its meaning is language-dependent. However, the UML provides three (rather hard to remember) abbreviations for visibility: + (public), − (private), and # (protected).

I'm tempted to leave it at that, but unfortunately, people draw diagrams that use visibility in specific ways. Therefore, to really understand some of the common differences that exist among models, you need to understand the approaches that different languages take to visibility. So, let's take a deep breath and dive into the murk.

We start with C++, because it's the basis for standard UML usage.

- A public member is visible anywhere in the program and may be called by any object within the system.
- A private member may be used only by the class that defines it.
- A protected member may be used only by (a) the class that defines it or (b) a subclass of that class.

Consider a Customer class that has a Personal Customer subclass. Consider also the object Martin, which is an instance of Personal Customer. Martin can use any public member of any object in the system. Martin may also use any private member of the class Personal Customer. Martin may *not* use any private members defined within Customer; Martin may, however, use protected members of Customer and protected users of Personal Customer.

Now look at Smalltalk. Within that language, all instance variables are private, and all operations are public. However, private doesn't mean the same thing in Smalltalk that it does in C++. In a Smalltalk system, Martin can access any instance variable within his own object whether that instance variable was defined within Customer or Personal Customer. So, in a sense, private in Smalltalk is similar to protected in C++.

Ah, but that would be too simple.

Let's go back to C++. Say I have another instance of Personal Customer, called Kendall. Kendall can access any member of Martin that was defined as part of the Personal Customer class, whether public, private, or protected. Kendall may also access any protected or public member of Martin that was defined within Customer. However, in Smalltalk, Kendall cannot access Martin's private instance variables— only Martin's public operations.

In C++, you may access members of other objects of your own class in the same way that you access your own members. In Smalltalk, it makes no difference whether another object is of the same class or not; you can access only public parts of another object.

I prefer not to access private or protected members of other objects of the same class. Many others follow this (unstated) convention.

Java is similar to C++ in that it offers free access to members of other objects of one's own class. Java also adds a new visibility level called package. A member with package visibility may be accessed only by instances of other classes within the same package.

In keeping with our theme, to ensure that things are not too simple, Java slightly redefines protected visibility. In Java, a protected member may be accessed by subclasses but also by any other class in the same package as the owning class. This means that in Java, protected is more public than package.

Java also allows classes to be marked public or package. A public class's public members may be used by any class that imports the package to which the class belongs. A package class may be used only by other classes in the same package.

C++ adds a final twist. One C++ method or class can be made a friend of a class. A **friend** has complete access to all members of a class—hence, the phrase "in C++, friends touch each other's private parts."

When you are using visibility, use the rules of the language in which you are working. When you are looking at a UML model from elsewhere, be wary of the meanings of the visibility markers, and be aware of how those meanings can change from language to language.

I usually find that visibilities change as you work with the code, so don't get too hung up on them early on.

Class Scope Features

You can define operations or attributes at class scope. This means that they are features of the class, rather than of each object. These operations or attributes correspond to static members in C++ or Java and to class methods or variables in Smalltalk. You show them just the same as any other operation or attribute, except that you <u>underline</u> them.

Chapter 6

Interaction Diagrams

Interaction diagrams are models that describe how groups of objects collaborate in some behavior.

Typically, an interaction diagram captures the behavior of a single use case. The diagram shows a number of example objects and the messages that are passed between these objects within the use case.

I'll illustrate the approach with a simple use case that exhibits the following behavior.

- The Order Entry window sends a "prepare" message to an Order.

- The Order then sends "prepare" to each Order Line on the Order.

- Each Order Line checks the given Stock Item.

  — If this check returns "true," the Order Line removes the appropriate quantity of Stock Item from stock.

  — Otherwise, the quantity of Stock Item has fallen below the reorder level, and that Stock Item requests a new delivery.

There are two kinds of interaction diagrams: sequence diagrams and collaboration diagrams.

Sequence Diagrams

Within a **sequence diagram**, an object is shown as a box at the top of a dashed vertical line (see Figure 6-1).

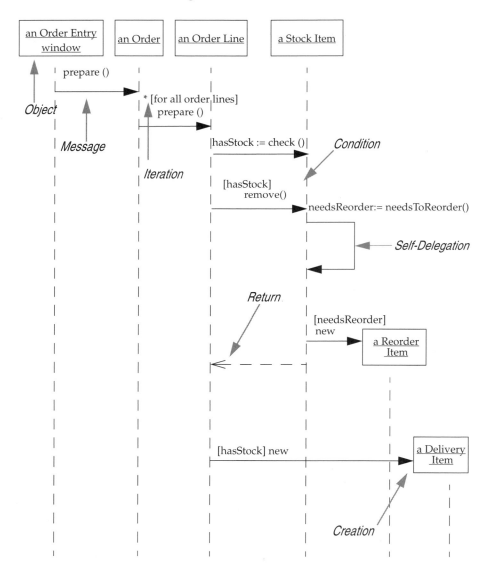

Figure 6-1: *Sequence Diagram*

This vertical line is called the object's **lifeline**. The lifeline represents the object's life during the interaction. This form was first popularized by Jacobson.

Each message is represented by an arrow between the lifelines of two objects. The order in which these messages occur is shown top to bottom on the page. Each message is labeled at minimum with the message name; you can also include the arguments and some control information, and you can show **self-delegation**, a message that an object sends to itself, by sending the message arrow back to the same lifeline.

Two bits of control information are valuable. First, there is a **condition**, which indicates when a message is sent (for example, *[needsReorder]*). The message is only sent if the condition is true. The second useful control marker is the **iteration marker**, which shows that a message is sent many times to multiple receiver objects, as would happen when you are iterating over a collection. You can show the basis of iteration within brackets (such as *[for all order lines]).

As you can see, Figure 6-1 is very simple and has immediate visual appeal. This is its great strength.

One of the hardest things to understand in an object-oriented program is the overall flow of control. A good design has lots of small methods in different classes, and at times it can be tricky to figure out the overall sequence of behavior. You can end up looking at the code trying to find the program. This is particularly true for those new to objects. Sequence diagrams help you to see that sequence.

This diagram includes a **return**, which indicates the return from a message, not a new message. Returns differ from the regular messages in that the line is dashed.

The POSA diagrams (Buschmann *et al.* 1996), on which much of the UML sequence chart notation is based, use returns extensively. I do not. I find that returns add a lot of clutter to a diagram and tend to obscure the flow. All returns are implied by the way the messages are sequenced. I only use returns on those occasions when they improve the clarity of the diagram.

My advice is to show returns only when they improve clarity. The only reason I used a return in Figure 6-1 is to demonstrate the notation; if you remove the return, I think the diagram remains just as clear.

In UML 1.0, returns were indicated by feathered arrowheads rather than dashed lines. I found that so difficult to implement that I used dashed lines anyway, so I'm glad to see the change.

I mention this because I'd like to offer a piece of general advice here: Be very wary of going against the UML notation. This notation will become a well-understood notation, and to do something non-standard will harm your communication with other designers. If something is causing painful confusion, however, I would do something non-standard. After all, the primary purpose of the diagram is communication. If you do break the UML's rules, do it sparingly and clearly define what you have done.

Concurrent Processes and Activations

Sequence diagrams are also valuable for concurrent processes.

In Figure 6-2, we see some objects that are checking a bank transaction.

When a Transaction is created, it creates a Transaction Coordinator to coordinate the checking of the Transaction. This coordinator creates a number (in this case, two) of Transaction Checker objects, each of which is responsible for a particular check. This process would make it easy to add different checking processes because each checker is called asynchronously and proceeds in parallel.

When a Transaction Checker completes, it notifies the Transaction Coordinator. The coordinator looks to see if all the checkers called back. If not, the coordinator does nothing. If they have, and all of them are successful, as in this case, then the coordinator notifies the Transaction that all is well.

Figure 6-2 introduces a number of new elements to sequence diagrams. First, you see **activations**, which appear explicitly when a method is active because it is either executing or waiting for a subroutine to return. Many designers use activations all the time. I find they don't add much to procedural execution, so I use them only in concurrent situations.

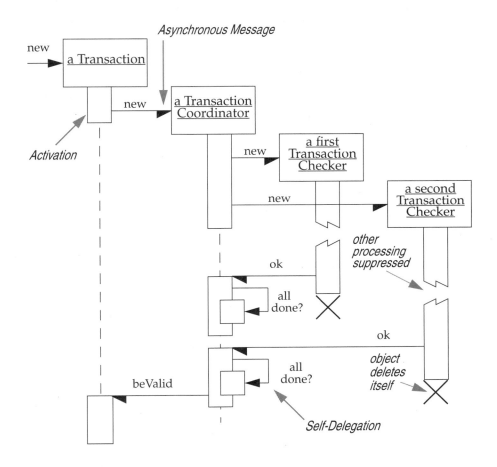

Figure 6-2: *Concurrent Processes and Activations*

The half-arrowheads indicate an **asynchronous** message. An asynchronous message does not block the caller, so it can carry on with its own processing. An asynchronous message can do one of three things.

1. Create a new thread, in which case it links to the top of an activation

2. Create a new object

3. Communicate with a thread that is already running

Object **deletion** is shown with a large X. Objects can self-destruct (shown in Figure 6-2), or they can be destroyed by another message (see Figure 6-3).

You can show the consequences of self-delegation more clearly when you have activations. Without them, or without the stacking notation used here, it is hard to tell where further calls occur after a self-delegation—either in the calling method or the called method. The stacking activations make this clear. I sometimes find this is a reason to use activations in a procedural interaction, even though I don't usually use activations in these cases.

Figures 6-2 and 6-3 show two of the scenarios in the "transaction checking" use case. I have drawn each scenario separately. There are techniques for combining the conditional logic onto a single diagram, but I prefer not to use them because it makes the diagram too complicated.

In Figure 6-3, I've employed a very useful technique: I've inserted textual descriptions of what's happening along the left side of the sequence diagram. This involves lining up each text block with the appropriate message within the diagram. This helps in understanding the diagram (at the cost of some extra work). I do this for documents I'm going to keep but not for whiteboard sketches.

Collaboration Diagrams

The second form of the interaction diagram is the **collaboration diagram**.

Within a collaboration diagram, the example objects are shown as icons. As on a sequence diagram, arrows indicate the messages sent within the given use case. This time, however, the sequence is indicated by numbering the messages.

Numbering the messages makes it more difficult to see the sequence than putting the lines down the page. On the other hand, the spatial layout allows you to show other things more easily. You can show how the objects are linked together and use the layout to overlay packages or other information.

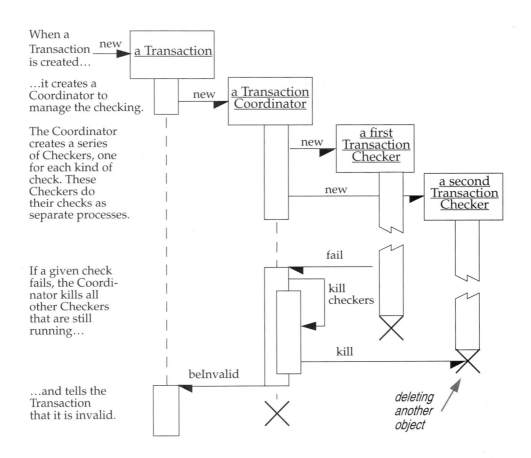

Figure 6-3: *Sequence Diagram: Check Failure*

You can use one of several numbering schemes for collaboration diagrams. The simplest is illustrated in Figure 6-4. Another approach involves a decimal numbering scheme, seen in Figure 6-5.

In the past, most people used the simple numbering scheme. The UML uses the decimal scheme because it makes it clear which operation is calling which other operation, although it can be harder to see the overall sequence.

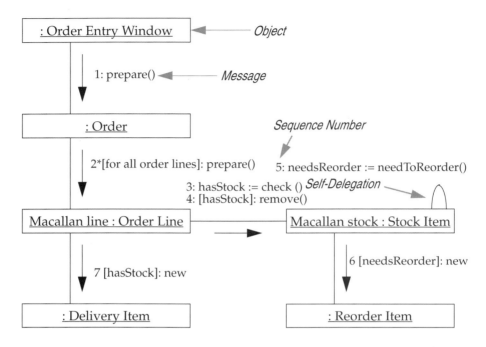

Figure 6-4: *Collaboration Diagram with Simple Numbering*

Regardless of what numbering scheme you use, you can add the same kind of control information you might show on a sequence diagram.

In Figures 6-4 and 6-5, you can see the various forms of the UML's object naming scheme. This takes the form *objectName : ClassName*, where either the object name or the class name may be omitted. Note that if you omit the object name, you must retain the colon so that it is clear that it is the class name and not the object name. So the name "Macallan line : Order Line" indicates an instance of Order Line called Macallan line (this is an order I would particularly appreciate). I tend to name objects in the Smalltalk style that I used in the sequence diagrams. (This scheme is legal UML because "anObject" is a perfectly good name for an object.)

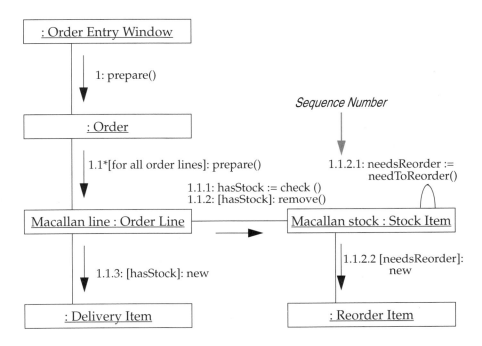

Figure 6-5: *Collaboration Diagram with Decimal Numbering*

Comparing Sequence and Collaboration Diagrams

Different developers have different preferences when it comes to choosing the form of interaction diagram to use. I usually prefer the sequence diagram because I like the emphasis it puts on sequence; it is easy to see the order in which things occur. Others prefer the collaboration diagram because they can use the layout to indicate how objects are statically connected.

One of the principal features of either form of an interaction diagram is its simplicity. You can easily see the messages by looking at the diagram. However, if you try to represent something other than a single sequential process without much conditional or looping behavior, the technique begins to break down.

Conditional Behavior

What is the best way to show a lot of conditional behavior?

There are two schools of thought. One is to use separate diagrams for each scenario. The other is to use conditions on messages to indicate the behavior.

I prefer the former. Interaction diagrams are at their best when the behavior is simple; they quickly lose their clarity with more complex behavior. If I want to capture complex behavior in a single diagram, I prefer to use an activity diagram (see Chapter 9).

The UML provides a lot of additional syntax for sequence diagrams, based on the work of the patterns team at Siemens (Buschmann *et al.* 1996). I won't go into it in detail here, mainly because I'm not too keen on the complexity it encourages. To me, the beauty of interaction diagrams is their simplicity, and many of the additional notations lose it in their drive to computational completeness. I encourage you not to rush to the more complex forms of interaction diagrams, because you may find the simpler ones provide the best value.

When to Use Interaction Diagrams

You should use interaction diagrams when you want to look at the behavior of several objects within a single use case. They are good at showing collaborations among the objects; they are not so good at precise definition of the behavior.

If you want to look at the behavior of a single object across many use cases, use a state transition diagram (see Chapter 8). If you want to look at behavior across many use cases or many threads, consider an activity diagram (see Chapter 9).

Where to Find Out More

Buschmann *et al.* (1996) uses many extensions that are currently in the mix for the UML and should give you a good idea of what is in store.

Chapter 7

Package Diagrams

One of the oldest questions in software methods is: How do you break down a large system into smaller systems? We ask this question because as systems get large, it becomes difficult to understand them and the changes we make to them.

Structured methods used **functional decomposition**, in which the overall system was mapped as a function and broken down into subfunctions, which were broken down further into sub-sub-functions, and so forth. The functions were like the use cases in an object-oriented system in that functions represented something the system as a whole did.

Those were the days when process and data were separated. So in addition to a functional decomposition, there was also a data structure. This took second place, although some Information Engineering techniques grouped data records into subject areas and produced matrices to show how the functions and data records interacted.

It is from this viewpoint that we see the biggest change that objects have wrought. The separation of process and data is gone, functional decomposition is gone, but the old question still remains. One idea is to group the classes together into higher-level units. This idea, applied very loosely, appears in many object methods. In the UML, this grouping mechanism is called the **package**.

The idea of a package can be applied to any model element, not just classes. Without some heuristics to group classes together, the grouping becomes arbitrary. The one I have found most useful and the one stressed most in the UML is the dependency. I use the term **package diagram** for a diagram that shows packages of classes and the dependencies among them.

Strictly speaking, packages and dependencies are elements on a class diagram, so a package diagram is just a form of class diagram. In practice, I find I draw these diagrams for different reasons, so I like to use different names.

A **dependency** exists between two elements if changes to the definition of one element may cause changes to the other. With classes, dependencies exist for various reasons: One class sends a message to another; one class has another as part of its data; one class mentions another as a parameter to an operation. If a class changes its interface, then any message it sends may no longer be valid.

Ideally, only changes to a class's interface should affect any other class. The art of large-scale design involves minimizing dependencies—that way, the effects of change are reduced and the system requires less effort to change.

In Figure 7-1, we have domain classes that model the business, grouped into two packages: Orders and Customers. Both packages are part of an overall domain package. The Order Capture application has dependencies with both domain packages. The Order Capture UI has dependencies with the Order Capture application and the AWT (a Java GUI toolkit).

A dependency between two packages exists if any dependency exists between any two classes in the packages. For example, if any class in the Mailing List package is dependent on any class in the Customers package, then a dependency exists between their corresponding packages.

There is an obvious similarity between package dependencies and compilation dependencies. In fact, there is a vital difference: With packages, the dependencies are not transitive.

An example of a **transitive** relationship is one in which Jim has a larger beard than Grady, and Grady has a larger beard than Ivar, so we can deduce that Jim has a larger beard than Ivar. Other examples include relationships such as "is north of" and "is taller than." On the other hand, "is a friend of" is not a transitive relationship.

To see why this is important for dependencies, look at Figure 7-1 again. If a class in the Orders package changes, this does not indicate that the Order Capture UI package needs to be changed. It merely indicates that the Order Capture application package needs to be looked at to see if it changes. Only if the Order Capture application package's interface is altered does the Order Capture UI package need to change. In this case, the Order Capture application is shielding the Order Capture UI from changes to orders.

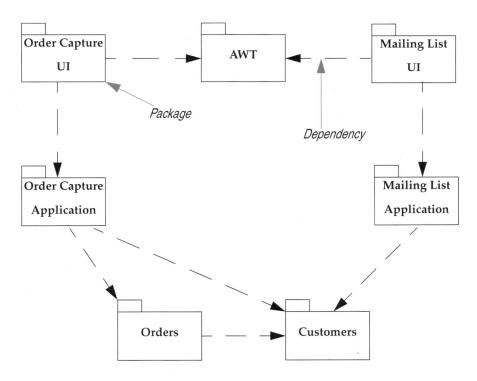

Figure 7-1: *Package Diagram*

This behavior is the classic purpose of a layered architecture. Indeed, these are the semantics of the Java "imports" behavior but not that of the C/C++ "includes" behavior nor that of Envy's prerequisites. The

C/C++ includes is transitive, which means that the Order Capture UI would be dependent on the Orders package. A transitive dependency makes it difficult to limit the scope of changes with compilation.

What does it mean to draw a dependency to a package that contains subpackages? Designers use different conventions. Some assume that drawing a dependency to a "containing" package gives visibility to the contents of all contained packages and their contents. Others say that you only see classes within the containing package, not classes within nested packages (that is, the view is opaque).

You should state which convention you are using within your project or make it clear by putting stereotypes on the packages. I suggest you use the «transparent» stereotype to indicate that you can see into nested packages and use the «opaque» stereotype to indicate that you can't. My convention here is that packages are transparent.

What do you see if you have a dependency into a package? Essentially, you see all public classes in the package and all of their public methods. Under the visibility scheme of C++, this can lead to a problem because you may want a class that contains methods that can be seen by other objects within the same package but not by objects that belong to other packages.

This is why Java has the package visibility. Obviously, this makes it easy for Java. You can mark classes and operations with package visibility within C++. Even though that convention will not be enforced by the compiler, it is still useful in design.

A useful technique here is to reduce the interface of the package further by exporting only a small subset of the operations associated with the package's classes. You can do this by giving all classes package visibility so that they can only be seen by other classes in the same package and by adding extra public classes for the public behavior. These extra classes, called *Facades* (Gamma *et al.* 1994), then delegate public operations to their shyer companions in the package.

Packages do not offer answers about how to reduce dependencies in your system, but they do help you to see what the dependencies are—and you can only work to reduce dependencies when you can see them. Package diagrams are a key tool for me in maintaining control over a system's overall structure.

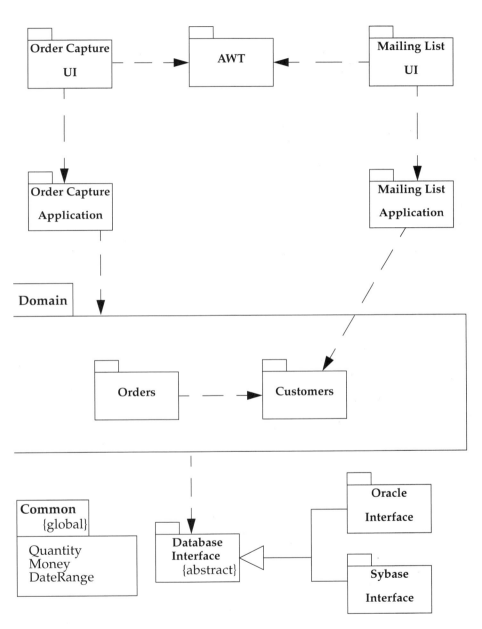

Figure 7-2: *Advanced Package Diagram*

Figure 7-2 is a more complex package diagram that contains additional constructs.

First, we see that I have added a Domain package that contains the orders and customers packages. This is useful because it means I can draw dependencies to and from the overall package, instead of many separate dependencies.

When you show a package's contents, you put the name of the package in the "tab" and the contents inside the main box. These contents can be a list of classes (such as in the Common package), another package diagram (as in Domain), or a class diagram (not shown, but the idea should be obvious by now).

Most of the time, I find it sufficient to list the key classes, but sometimes a further diagram is useful. In this case, I've shown that while the Order Capture application has a dependency to the entire Domain package, the Mailing List application is dependent only on the Customers package. Strictly speaking, simply listing the classes isn't pure UML (you should show the class icons), but this is one of the areas in which I would be inclined to bend the rules.

Figure 7-2 shows the Common package marked as {global}. This means that all packages in the system have a dependency to Common. Obviously, you should use this construct sparingly, but common classes (such as Money) are used everywhere.

You can use generalization with packages. This means that the specific package must conform to the interface of the general package. This is comparable to the specification perspective of subtyping within class diagrams (see Chapter 4). Therefore, in accordance with Figure 7-2, the Database Broker can use either the Oracle Interface or the Sybase Interface. When generalization is used like this, the general package may be marked as {abstract} to show that it merely defines an interface that is implemented by a more specific package.

Generalization implies a dependency from the subtype to the supertype. (You don't need to show the extra dependency; the generalization itself is enough.) Putting abstract classes in a supertype package is a good way of breaking cycles in the dependency structure. In this situation, the database interface packages are responsible for loading and saving the domain objects in a database. They therefore need to know about the domain objects. However, the domain objects need to trigger the loading and saving.

The generalization allows us to put the necessary triggering interface (various load and save operations) into the database interface package. These operations are then implemented by classes within the subtype packages. We don't need a dependency between the database interface package and the Oracle interface package, because at run time it will actually be the subtype package that gets called by the domain. But the domain only thinks it is dealing with the (simpler) database interface package. Polymorphism is just as useful for packages as it is for classes.

As a rule of thumb, it is a good idea to remove cycles in the dependency structure. I'm not convinced that you can remove all cycles, but you should certainly minimize them. If you do have them, try to contain them within a larger containing package. In practice, I have found cases in which I have not been able to avoid cycles between domain packages, but I do try to eliminate them from the interactions between the domain and external interfaces. Package generalization is a key element in doing this.

In an existing system, dependencies can be inferred by looking at the classes. This is a very useful task for a tool to perform. I find this handy if I am trying to improve the structure of an existing system. A useful early step is to divide the classes into packages and to analyze the dependences among the packages. Then I refactor to reduce the dependencies.

When to Use Package Diagrams

Packages are a vital tool for large projects. Use them whenever a class diagram that encompasses the whole system is no longer legible on a single letter-size (or A4) sheet of paper.

You want to keep your dependencies to a minimum since this reduces coupling. However, the heuristics for this are not well understood.

Packages are particularly useful for testing. Although I do write some tests on a class by class basis, I prefer to do my unit testing on a package by package basis. Each package should have one or more test classes that test the behavior of the package.

Where to Find Out More

The original source for packages was Grady Booch (1994); he called them class categories. His treatment was very brief, however. The best discussion I know of this subject is by Robert Martin (1995), whose book gives several examples of using Booch and C++, with a lot of attention paid to minimizing dependencies. You can also find valuable information in Wirfs-Brock (1990); the author refers to packages as subsystems.

Chapter 8

State Diagrams

State diagrams are a familiar technique to describe the behavior of a system. They describe all the possible states a particular object can get into and how the object's state changes as a result of events that reach the object. In most OO techniques, state diagrams are drawn for a single class to show the lifetime behavior of a single object.

There are many forms of state diagrams, each with slightly different semantics. The most popular one used in OO techniques is based on David Harel's statechart (Vol. 8). It was first used for OO methods by OMT and adopted by Grady Booch in his second edition (1994).

Figure 8-1 shows a UML state diagram for an order in the order processing system I introduced earlier in the book. The diagram indicates the various states of an order.

We begin at the start point and show an initial transition into the Checking state. This transition is labeled "/get first item." The syntax for a transition label has three parts, all of which are optional: *Event [Guard] / Action*. In this case, we have only the action "get first item." Once we perform that action, we enter the Checking state. This state has an activity associated with it, indicated by a label with the syntax *do/activity*. In this case, the activity is called "check item."

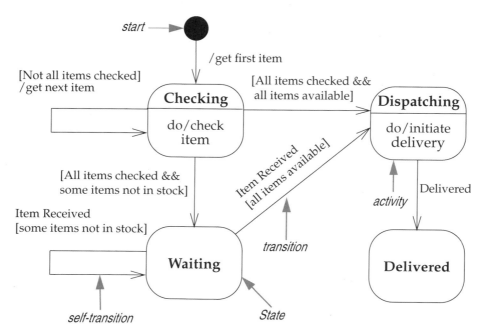

Figure 8-1: *State Diagram*

Notice that I used the terms "action" for the transition and "activity" for the state. Although they are both processes, typically implemented by some method on Order, they are treated differently. **Actions** are associated with transitions and are considered to be processes that occur quickly and are not interruptible. **Activities** are associated with states and can take longer. An activity may be interrupted by some event.

Note that the definition of "quickly" depends on the kind of system you are producing. Within a hard real-time system, "quickly" may mean within a few machine instructions; for regular information systems, "quickly" might mean less than a few seconds.

When a transition has no event within its label, it means that the transition occurs as soon as any activity associated with the given state is completed. In this case, that means as soon as we are done with the Checking. Three transitions come out of the Checking state. All three have only guards on their label. A **guard** is a logical condition that will return only "true" or "false." A guarded transition occurs only if the guard resolves to "true."

Only one transition can be taken out of a given state, so we intend the guards to be mutually exclusive for any event. in Figure 8-1, we address three conditions.

1.   If we have not checked all items, we get the next item and return to the Checking state to check it.

2.   If we have checked all items and they were all in stock, we transition to the Dispatching state.

3.   If we have checked all items but not all of them were in stock, we transition to the Waiting state.

I'll look at the Waiting state first. There are no activities for this state, so the given order sits in this state waiting for an event. Both transitions out of the Waiting state are labeled with the Item Received event. This means that the order waits until it detects this event. At that point, it evaluates the guards on the transitions and makes the appropriate transition (either to Dispatching or back to Waiting).

Within the Dispatching state, we have an activity that initiates a delivery. There is also a single, unguarded transition triggered by the Delivered event. This indicates that the transition will always occur when that event occurs. Note, however, that the transition does *not* occur when the activity completes; instead, once the "initiate delivery" activity is finished, the given order remains in the Dispatching state until the Delivered event occurs.

The final thing to address is a transition named "cancelled." We want to be able to cancel an order at any point before it is delivered. We could do this by drawing separate transitions from each of the Checking, Waiting, and Dispatching states. A useful alternative is to create a **superstate** of all three states and then draw a single transition from that. The substates simply inherit any transitions on the superstate.

Figures 8-2 and 8-3 show how these approaches reflect the same system behavior. Even with only three duplicated transitions, Figure 8-2 looks rather cluttered. Figure 8-3 makes the whole picture much clearer, and if changes are needed later, it is harder to forget the cancelled event.

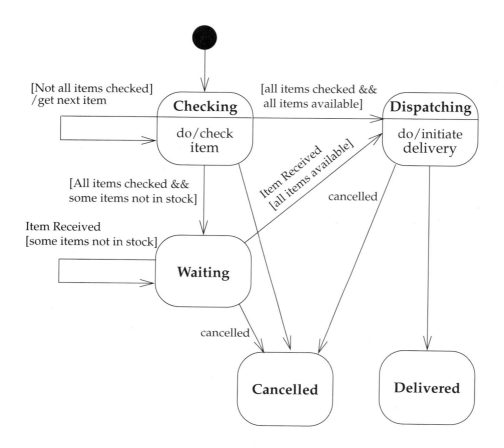

Figure 8-2: *State Diagram Without Superstates*

In the current examples, I have shown an activity within a state, indicated by text in the form *do/activity*. You can also indicate other things within a state.

If a state responds to an event with an action that does not cause a transition, you can show this by putting text in the form *eventName / actionName* in the state box.

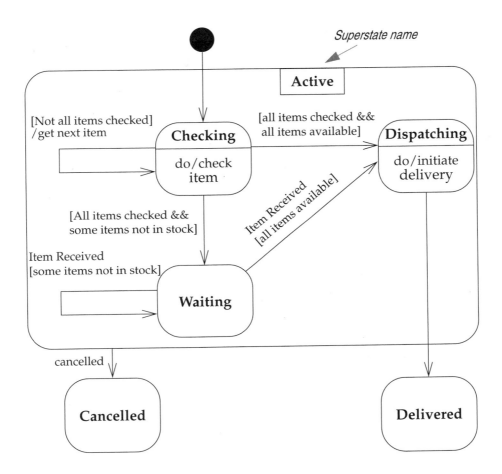

Figure 8-3: *State Diagram with Superstates*

There are also two special events, entry and exit. Any action that is marked as linked to the **entry** event is executed whenever the given state is entered via a transition. The action associated with the **exit** event is executed whenever the state is left via a transition. If you have a transition that goes back to the same state (this is called a **self-transition**) with an action, the exit action would be executed first, then the transition's action, and finally the entry action. If the state has an associated activity, as well, that activity is executed after the entry action.

Concurrent State Diagrams

In addition to states of an order that are based on the availability of the items, there are also states that are based on payment authorization. If we look at these states, we might see a state diagram like the one in Figure 8-4.

Here we begin by doing an authorization. The "check payment" activity finishes by signaling that the payment is approved. If the payment is OK, the given order waits in the Authorized state until the "deliver" event occurs. Otherwise, the order enters the Rejected state.

The Order object exhibits a combination of the behaviors shown in Figures 8-1 and 8-2. The associated states and the Cancelled state discussed earlier can be combined on a **concurrent state diagram** (see Figure 8-5).

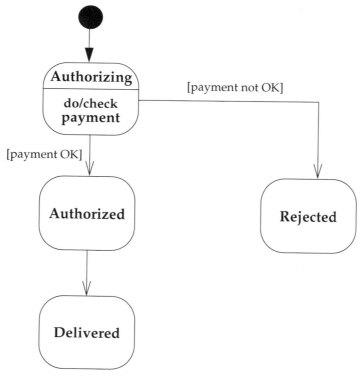

Figure 8-4: *Payment Authorization*

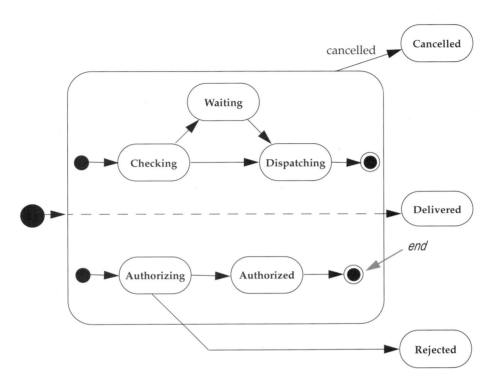

Figure 8-5: *Concurrent State Diagram*

Note that in Figure 8-5, I left out details of the internal states.

The concurrent sections of the state diagram are places in which at any point, the given order is in two different states, one from each diagram. When the order leaves the concurrent states, it is only in a single state. We can see that an order starts off in both the Checking and Authorizing states. If the "check payment" activity of the Authorizing state completes successfully first, then the order will be in the Checking and Authorized states. If the "cancel" event occurs, then the order will be in only the Cancelled state.

Concurrent state diagrams are useful when a given object has sets of independent behaviors. Note, however, that you should not get too many concurrent sets of behaviors occurring in a single object. If you have several complicated concurrent state diagrams for an object, you should consider splitting the object into separate objects.

When to Use State Diagrams

State diagrams are good at describing the behavior of an object across several use cases. They are not very good at describing behavior that involves a number of objects collaborating together. As such, it is useful to combine state diagrams with other techniques. For instance, interaction diagrams (see Chapter 6) are good at describing the behavior of several objects in a single use case, and activity diagrams (see Chapter 9) are good at showing the general sequence of actions for several objects and use cases.

Some people find state diagrams natural, but many find them unnatural. Keep an eye on how people are working with them—it may be that your team does not find state diagrams useful to their way of working. That is not a big problem; as always, you should remember to use the mix of techniques that works for you.

If you do use state diagrams, don't try to draw them for every class in the system. Although this approach is often used by high-ceremony completists, it is almost always a waste of effort. Use state diagrams only for those classes that exhibit interesting behavior, where building the state diagram helps you understand what is going on. Many people find that UI and control objects have the kind of behavior that is useful to depict with a state diagram.

Where to Find Out More

Both Grady Booch (1994) and Jim Rumbaugh (1991) have material on state diagrams, although neither contains much more detail than appears in this chapter. The most detailed treatment of statecharts is in Cook and Daniels (1994), a book I strongly recommend if you often use statecharts. The semantics they define are much more detailed than in other books. Although those semantics may not be entirely consistent with UML semantics, the authors do go into detailed issues that you should be aware of if you are using state diagrams.

Chapter 9

Activity Diagrams

Activity diagrams are one of most unexpected parts of the UML.

Unlike most other techniques in the UML, the activity diagram doesn't have clear origins in the previous works of the three amigos. The **activity diagram** combines ideas from several techniques: the event diagrams of Jim Odell, SDL state modeling techniques, and Petri nets. These diagrams are particularly useful in connection with workflow and in describing behavior that has a lot of parallel processing.

In Figure 9-1, which comes from the UML 1.0 documentation, the core symbol is the **activity**. The interpretation of this term depends on the perspective from which you are drawing the diagram. In a conceptual diagram, an activity is some task that needs to be done, whether by a human or a computer. In a specification-perspective diagram or an implementation-perspective diagram, an activity is a method on a class.

Each activity can be followed by another activity. This is simple sequencing. For example, in Figure 9-1, the Put Coffee in Filter activity is followed by the Put Filter in Machine activity. So far, the activity diagram looks like a flowchart. We can explore the differences by looking at the Find Beverage activity.

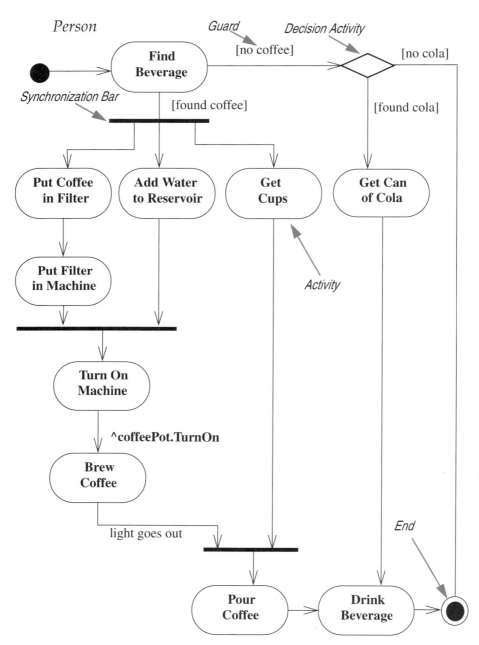

Figure 9-1: *Activity Diagram*

Find Beverage has two triggers coming out of it. Each trigger has a **guard**, a logical expression that evaluates to "true" or "false" just as on a state diagram (see Chapter 8). In the case of Figure 8-1, the person will follow the Find Beverage activity by thinking about coffee or cola.

We'll assume that we can find a bag of Peet's New Guinea and go down the coffee route. This trigger leads to a **synchronization bar**, attached to which are three outgoing triggers. These triggers go to the Put Coffee in Filter, Add Water to Reservoir, and Get Cups activities, respectively.

The diagram says that these three activities can occur in parallel. Essentially, this means that their order is irrelevant. I could put coffee in the filter first, then add water to the reservoir, and then get the cups, or I could get the cups, then add the coffee to the filter—you get the picture.

I can also do these activities by interleaving. I could get a cup, add some water to the reservoir, get another cup, get some more water, and so forth. Or I could do some of this simultaneously: pour the water in with one hand while I reach for a cup with another. Any of these is correct, according to the diagram.

The activity diagram allows me to choose what order in which to do things. In other words, it merely states the essential sequencing rules I have to follow. This is the key difference between an activity diagram and a flowchart. Flowcharts are normally limited to sequential processes; activity diagrams can handle parallel processes.

This is important for business modeling. Businesses often have unnecessarily sequential processes. A technique like this that encourages parallel behavior is valuable in these situations because it encourages people to move away from unnecessary sequences in their behavior and to spot opportunities to do things in parallel. This can improve the efficiency and responsiveness of business processes.

Activity diagrams are also useful for concurrent programs since you can graphically lay out what threads you have and when they need to synchronize.

When you get parallel behavior, you need to synchronize. We don't want to turn on the coffee machine until we have put the filter in the machine and water in the reservoir. This is why we see the outbound triggers from these activities coming together in a synchronization bar. A plain synchronization bar like this indicates that the outbound trigger occurs only when both inbound triggers have occurred. As we will see later, these bars can be more complicated.

A further synchronization occurs later: The coffee has to be brewed and cups must be available before we can pour the coffee.

Now let's move on to the other track.

In this case, we have a compound decision. The first decision is about coffee, which governs the two triggers coming out of the Find Beverage. If there is no coffee, we are faced with a second decision, this one based on cola.

When we have decisions like this, we mark the second decision with a decision diamond. This allows us to describe nested decisions. We can have any number of nested decisions.

The Drink activity has two triggers coming into it, which means that it is performed in either case. For the moment, you can think of this as an OR case (I do it if one trigger or the other occurs) and the synchronization bar as the AND case (I do it if one trigger and the other occurs).

Activity Diagrams for Use Cases

Figure 9-1 describes a method on the type Person. Activity diagrams are useful for describing complicated methods. They can also be used elsewhere—for instance, to describe a use case.

Consider a use case for order processing.

> *When we receive an order, we check each line item on the order to see if we have the goods in stock. If we do, we assign the goods to the order. If this assignment sends the quantity of those goods in stock below the reorder level, we reorder the goods. While we are doing this, we check to see if the payment is OK. If the payment is OK and we have the goods in stock,*

*we dispatch the order. If the payment is OK but we don't have
the goods, we leave the order waiting. If the payment isn't
OK, we cancel the order.*

See Figure 9-2 for a visual representation of this use case.

This figure introduces a new construct to the activity diagram. Take a
look at the incoming trigger associated with the Check Line Item activity.
It is marked with a *. This is a multiplicity marker (the same
marker used in class diagrams; see Chapter 4) to show that when we
receive an order, we have to carry out the Check Line Item activity for
each line item on the order. This means that the Receive Order activity
is followed by one invocation of the Authorize Payment activity and
multiple invocations of the Check Line Item activity. All of these invocations
occur in parallel.

This highlights the second source of parallelism in an activity diagram.
You can get parallel activities through multiple transitions coming out
of a synchronization bar; you can also get parallel activities when the
same activity is triggered through a **multiple trigger**. Whenever you
have a multiple trigger, you should indicate on the diagram what the
basis of the trigger is, as in this case with [for each item on].

When you see a multiple trigger, you usually see a synchronization
bar, farther down in the diagram, that brings the parallel threads
together. In this case, we see this bar before the Dispatch Order activity.
The synchronization bar has a condition applied to it. Each time a
trigger comes to the synchronization bar, the condition is tested. If the
condition is true, the outbound trigger occurs. (You can also use
another * to indicate the threads coming together. I prefer not to show
a second * as it makes the diagram too confusing. I find that the synchronization
condition makes things clear.)

Unlabeled synchronization bars work in the same way. The lack of a
condition means that the default condition for synchronization bars is
used. The default is that all incoming triggers have occurred. That's
why there were no conditions on the bars in Figure 9-1.

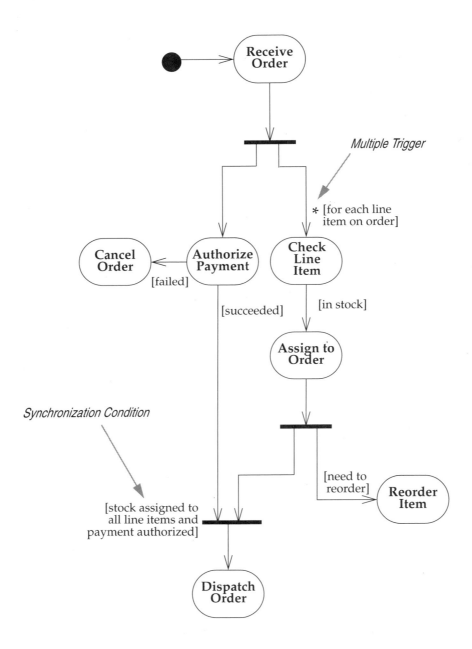

Figure 9-2: *Receiving an Order*

An activity diagram need not have a defined end point. The end point of an activity diagram is the point at which all the triggered activities have been run and there are no more left to do. On Figure 9-2, marking an explicit end point would not be helpful.

Figure 9-2 also has a dead end: the Reorder Item activity. After this activity is performed, nothing more happens. Dead ends are fine on a non-terminating activity diagram like this. Sometimes, they are obvious, as for Reorder Item. At other times, they are not so obvious. Look at the Check Line Item activity. It has only one outbound trigger, which has a condition. What happens if the given line item isn't in stock? Nothing—the thread just stops there.

In our example, we cannot dispatch an order until we get an incoming delivery that replenishes the stock. This might be a separate use case.

> *When a supply delivery comes in, we look at the outstanding orders and decide which ones we can fill from this incoming supply. We then assign each of these to its appropriate orders. Doing this may release those orders for dispatching. We put the remaining goods into stock.*

Figure 9-3 is an activity diagram that represents this use case.

This second use case shows how the order can wait to be dispatched until we get another delivery.

When each of two use cases shows part of the whole picture, I find it useful to draw a combined diagram, like the one in Figure 9-4. This diagram shows the activity diagrams for both use cases superimposed on each other, so you can see how actions in one use case affect actions in the other. Such an activity diagram has multiple start points, which is perfectly fine as the activity diagram represents how the business reacts to multiple external events.

I find this ability of activity diagrams to show behavior that spans multiple use cases to be particularly helpful. Use cases give us slices of information about a domain viewed from the outside; when we look at the internal picture, we need to see the whole. Class diagrams (see Chapter 4) show us the whole picture of interconnected classes, and activity diagrams do the same for behavior.

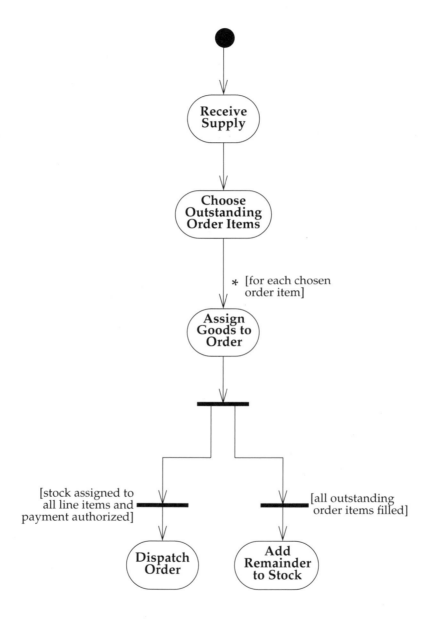

Figure 9-3: *Receiving Supply*

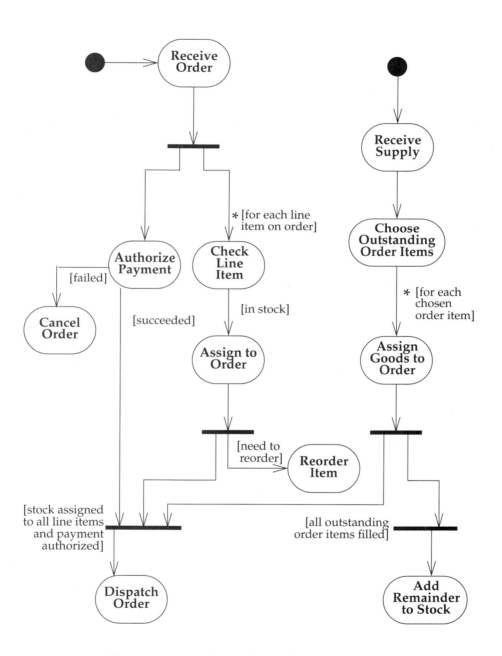

Figure 9-4: *Receive Order and Receive Supply*

Swimlanes

Activity diagrams tell you what happens, but they do not tell you who does what. In programming, this means that the diagram does not convey which class is responsible for each activity.

In domain modeling, this means that the diagram does not convey which people or departments are responsible for each activity. One way around this is to label each activity with the responsible class or human. This works, but does not offer the same clarity as interaction diagrams (see Chapter 6) for showing communication among objects.

Swimlanes are a way around this.

To use swimlanes, you must arrange your activity diagrams into vertical zones separated by lines. Each zone represents the responsibilities of a particular class or, in the case of Figure 9-5, a particular department.

Swimlanes are good in that they combine the activity diagram's depiction of logic with the interaction diagram's depiction of responsibility. However, they can be difficult to draw on a complex diagram. I have used non-linear zones on occasion, which is better than nothing. (Sometimes you have to stop trying to say too much in one diagram.)

Some people make sure to assign activities to objects when they draw an activity diagram. Others are happy to work with the activity diagram first, to get an overall sense of the behavior, and assign the activities to objects later. I've seen people who assign immediately get emotional about those who defer assignment; they make unpleasant accusations of drawing dataflow diagrams and not being object-oriented.

I confess I sometimes draw an activity diagram without assigning behavior to objects until later. I find it useful to figure out one thing at a time. This is particularly true when I'm doing business modeling and encouraging a domain expert to think of new ways of doing things. That way works for me. Others prefer to assign behavior to objects immediately. You should do whatever you're more comfortable doing. The important thing is to assign activities to classes before you are done. Often, I use an interaction diagram (see Chapter 6).

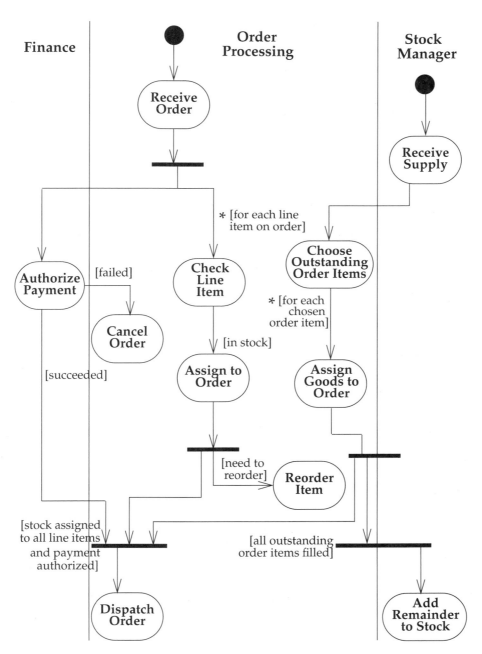

Figure 9-5: *Swimlanes*

Decomposing an Activity

An activity can be decomposed into further description. This description can be text, code, or another activity diagram (see Figure 9-6).

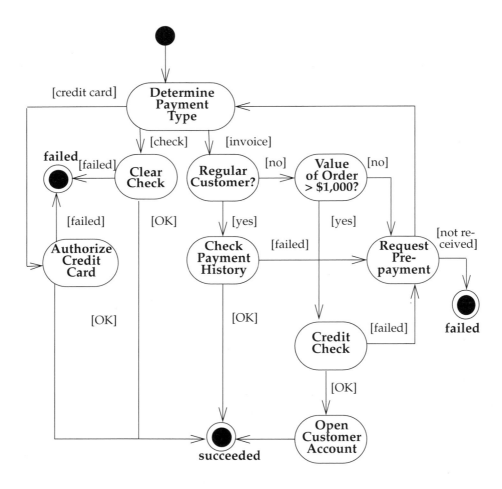

Figure 9-6: *Decomposed Activity Diagram*

When you draw an activity diagram as a decomposition of a higher-level activity, you must provide a single start point. You can, however, provide as many end points as there are outgoing triggers within the higher-level activity. This allows the subsidiary diagram to return a value that determines later triggering. For instance, Figure 9-6 shows the Authorize Credit Card activity, which returns either "succeeded" or "failed."

Figure 9-6 was drawn from a conceptual perspective, but it is not too difficult to imagine drawing this as a graphical portrayal of programming code, just like a flowchart. I tend not to do this, for the same reason that I don't draw flowcharts. It's usually easier to simply write the code. If you find graphics useful here, you might try this, particularly if you want to show multiple threads.

There are tools that can execute Odell's event diagrams, a precursor to activity diagrams. If you are using such a tool, you might find it valuable for prototyping.

If you have a lot of logic to represent, activity diagrams can easily become too tangled. In this situation, a truth table can be a better representation.

When to Use Activity Diagrams

Like most behavioral modeling techniques, activity diagrams have definite strengths and weaknesses, so they are best used in combination with other techniques.

The great strength of activity diagrams lies in the fact that they support and encourage parallel behavior. This makes them a great tool for workflow modeling and, in principle, for multi-threaded programming. Their great disadvantage is that they do not make the links among actions and objects very clear.

You can define what a relationship is by labeling an activity with an object name or by using swimlanes (which divide an activity diagram based on responsibilities), but this does not have the simple immediacy of interaction diagrams (see Chapter 6). For this reason, some people feel that using activity diagrams is not object-oriented and, thus, bad. I've found that the technique can be very useful, and I don't throw useful tools out of my toolkit.

I like to use activity diagrams in the following situations.

- *Analyzing a use case.* At this stage, I'm not interested in allocating actions to objects; I just need to understand what actions need to take place and what the behavioral dependencies are. I allocate methods to objects later and show those allocations with an interaction diagram.

- *Understanding workflow across many use cases.* When use cases interact with each other, activity diagrams are a great tool for representing and understanding that behavior. In situations that are dominated by workflow, I find them a superb tool.

- *Dealing with multi-threaded applications.* I have not used activity diagrams for this purpose, but they are well-suited to it.

Don't use activity diagrams in the following situations.

- *Trying to see how objects collaborate.* An interaction diagram is simpler and gives you a clearer picture of collaborations.

- *Trying to see how an object behaves over its lifetime.* Use a state diagram (see Chapter 8) for that.

Where to Find Out More

Activity diagrams are based on a number of workflow-oriented approaches. The most immediate ancestor is Jim Odell's event diagram, which you can find out more about in Martin and Odell's "foundations" book (1994).

Chapter 10

Deployment Diagrams

A **deployment diagram** shows the physical relationships among software and hardware components in the delivered system. A deployment diagram is a good place to show how components and objects are routed and move around a distributed system.

Each **node** on a deployment diagram represents some kind of computational unit—in most cases, a piece of hardware. The hardware may be a simple device or sensor, or it could be a mainframe.

Figure 10-1 shows a PC connected to a UNIX server through TCP/IP. **Connections** among nodes show the communication paths over which the system will interact.

Components on a deployment diagram represent physical modules of code. In my practice, these correspond exactly to the packages on a package diagram (see Chapter 7), so the deployment diagram shows where each package is running on the system.

The **dependencies** among the components should be the same as the package dependencies. These dependencies show how components communicate with other components. The direction of a given dependency indicates the knowledge in the communication.

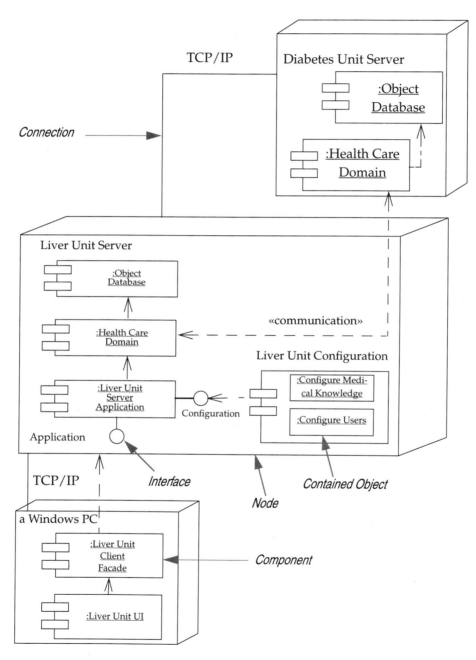

Figure 10-1: *Deployment Diagram*

So in the diagram, the Liver Unit UI is dependent on the Liver Unit Client Facade since it calls specific methods on the facade. Although the communication is two-way, in the sense that the Facade returns data, the Facade is not aware of who is calling it and is thus not dependent on the UI. In the communication between the two Health Care Domain components, both are aware that they are talking to another Health Care Domain component, so the communication dependency is two-way.

A component may have more than one interface, in which case you can see which components communicate with each interface. On Figure 9-1, the PC contains two components: the UI and the application facade. The application facade talks to the application interface of the server application. A separate configuration component runs only on the server. The application communicates with its local Health Care Domain component, which may communicate with other Health Care Domain components on the network.

The use of multiple Health Care Domain components is hidden from the application. Each Health Care Domain component has a local database.

When to Use Deployment Diagrams

In practice, I haven't seen this kind of a diagram used much. Most people do draw diagrams to show this kind of information, but they are informal cartoons. On the whole, I don't have a problem with that since each system has its own physical characteristics that you want to emphasize. As we wrestle more and more with distributed systems, however, I'm sure we will require more formality as we understand better which issues need to be highlighted in deployment diagrams.

Chapter 11

UML and Programming

So far, I have discussed a lot of notation. One large question looms: How does a programmer actually *use* the UML as part of the daily grind of programming? I'll answer this by talking about how I use the UML when I'm programming, even on a small scale. I won't go into a lot of detail, but I hope this will give you a sense of what you can do with the UML.

Let's imagine a computer system designed to pull together information about patients for a hospital.

Various health care professionals make observations about patients. This simple system will allow someone to get information about those observations and add additional observations. As this is a short book, I will wave my arms about the database links and the UI and only consider the basic domain classes.

This is such a simple example that it has but a single use case, named "review and add patient observations." We can elaborate on that with a few scenarios.

- Ask for the latest heart rate of a patient.
- Ask for the blood group of a patient.

- Update a patient's level of consciousness.
- Update a patient's heart rate. The system marks the rate as slow, normal, or fast, according to the system's built-in ranges.

My first step in the process is to come up with a conceptual model that describes the concepts in this domain. At this stage, I'm not thinking about how the software is going to work, only about how to organize concepts in the minds of the doctors and nurses. I'll start with a model based on several analysis patterns from Fowler (1997): *Observation, Quantity, Range,* and *Phenomenon with Range.*

Patient Observation: Domain Model

Figure 11-1 shows the initial domain model for our system.

How do these concepts represent the information in the domain?

I'll start with the simple concepts of Quantity, Unit, and Range. Quantity represents a dimensioned value, such as 6 feet—a quantity with amount of 6 and unit of feet. Units are simply those categories of measurement with which we want to deal. Range allows us to talk about ranges as a single concept—for instance, a range of 4 feet to 6 feet is represented as a single Range object with an upper bound of 6 feet and a lower bound of 4 feet. In general, ranges can be expressed in terms of anything that can be compared (using the operators <, >, <=, >=, and =), so the upper and lower bounds of a Range are both magnitudes. (Quantities are a kind of magnitude.)

Each observation made by a doctor or nurse is an instance of the Observation concept and is either a Measurement or a Category Observation. So a measurement of a height of 6 feet for Martin Fowler would be represented as an instance of Measurement. Associated with this Measurement are the amount 6 feet, the Phenomenon Type "height," and the Patient named Martin Fowler. Phenomenon Types represent the things that can be measured: height, weight, heart rate, and so forth.

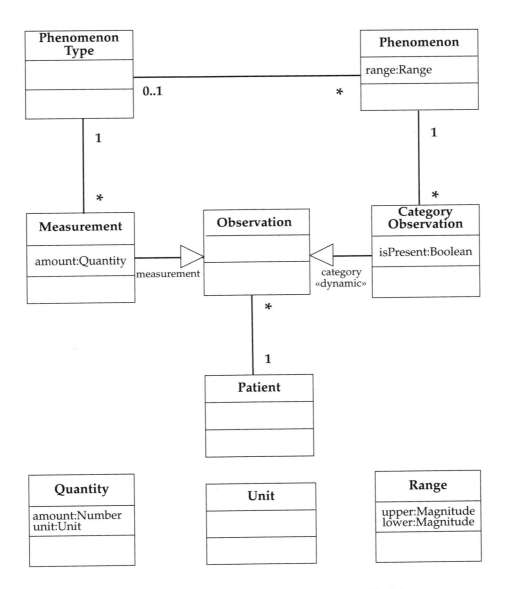

Figure 11-1: *Patient Observation Domain Model*

An observation that Martin Fowler's blood type is O would be represented as a Category Observation whose associated Phenomenon is "blood group O." This Phenomenon is linked to the Phenomenon Type "blood group."

Figure 11-2 should make things a little clearer at this point.

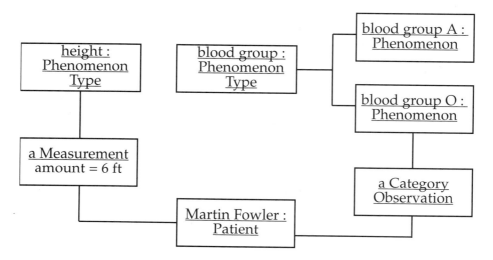

Figure 11-2: *Patient Observation Object Diagram*

Figure 11-3 shows that we can make an Observation serve as both a Measurement and a Category Observation by stating that a Measurement of "90 beats per minute" can also be a Category Observation whose associated Phenomenon is "fast heart rate."

At this stage, I have looked at only the representation of the concepts; I haven't thought much about behavior. I don't always do that, but it seems an appropriate starting point for a problem that is mainly about dealing with information.

For the moment, I'm still talking about patient observation *concepts*, just as I would be doing with a doctor or a nurse. (Indeed, that is what happened in real life. The conceptual models were built by a couple of doctors and a nurse, with me helping.) To make the move to an object-oriented program, I have to decide how to deal with the conceptual picture in terms of software. For this exercise, I have chosen the Java programming language. (I had to get Java into this book somehow!)

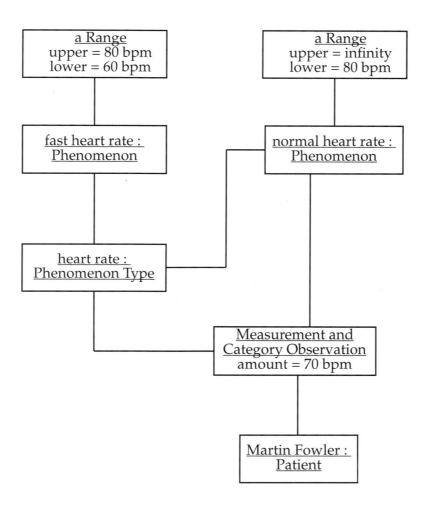

Figure 11-3: *Another Patient Observation Object Diagram*

Most of these concepts will work well as Java classes. Patient, Phenomenon Type, Phenomenon, Unit, and Quantity will work with no trouble. The two sticky items are Range and Observation.

Range is an issue because I want to form a range of quantities for a Phenomenon. I could do this by creating a "magnitude" interface and stating that Quantity implements that interface, but that would leave me with a lot of downcasting. This does not happen in Smalltalk, and I can use parameterized types in C++. For this exercise, I prefer to use a QuantityRange class that uses the *Range* pattern.

My problem with Observation is that an Observation can be both a Category Observation and a Measurement at the same time (see Figure 11-3). In Java, like most other programming languages, we have only single classification. I decided to deal with this by allowing any Observation to have an associated Phenomenon, which effectively lets the Observation class implement both the Observation and Category Observation concepts.

These decisions do not result in a perfect state of affairs, but they are the kind of pragmatic imperfection that allows work to get done. Don't try to do software that exactly maps the conceptual perspective. Try, instead, to be faithful to the spirit of conceptual perspective but still realistic considering the tools you are using.

Patient Observation: Specification Model

Figure 11-4 reflects modifications I made to the domain model to take into account some of the factors associated with a target language.

The patient observation model is now at the specification perspective. It shows the class interfaces rather than the classes themselves. I might keep the conceptual model for another day but, more likely, I will work only with the specification model from this point forward. I try not to keep too many models around. My rule of thumb is that if I cannot keep a model up to date, it goes in the bin. (I know I'm lazy, too!)

Now let's look at the *behavior* associated with our patient observation model.

The first scenario asks for the latest heart rate of the patient. The first question is: Whose responsibility is it to handle this request? The Patient seems the natural choice. The Patient needs to look at all its observations, determine which are measurements of the Phenomenon Type "heart rate," and find the latest value. To do this, I will have to add a timepoint to Measurement. Because this can apply to other observations, as well, I'll add it to Observation, too.

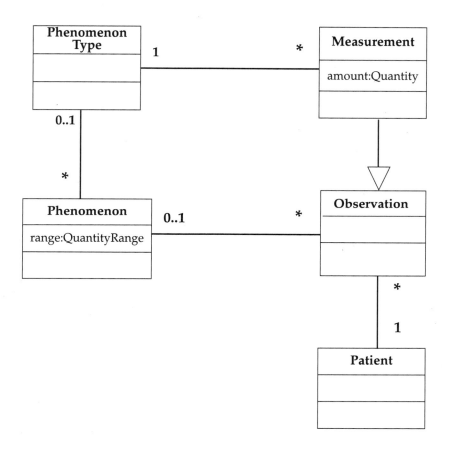

Figure 11-4: *Patient Observation Specification Model*

A similar responsibility exists for Phenomenon: Find the latest Category Observation that has a Phenomenon for the given Phenomenon Type.

Figure 11-5 shows operations that I've added to Patient to reflect my thinking.

Don't try too hard to come up with operations if they are not obvious just yet. The most important thing to go for is a statement of responsibility. If you can cast that in the form of an operation, that's fine; otherwise, a short phrase is useful in describing the responsibility.

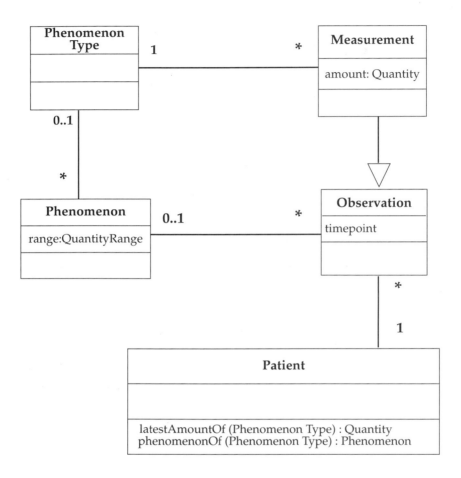

Figure 11-5: *Patient Observation Operations*

Updating the patient's level of consciousness involves creating a new Observation of the appropriate Phenomenon. In doing that, the user would usually like to pick a Phenomenon from a pop-up list of some kind. We can handle that by getting the Phenomenon objects associated with a particular Phenomenon Type as this responsibility is implied by the association between the two.

In adding a measurement, we need to create a new Measurement. Some additional complication comes from the fact that the Measurement needs to look to see if there is a Phenomenon that can be assigned. Here the Measurement can ask its associated Phenomenon Type if there is a Phenomenon to assign.

There is some collaboration among the objects here, which suggests that this is a good place for a sequence diagram (see Figure 11-6).

Do you *have* to draw all of these diagrams?

Not necessarily. Much depends on how well you can visualize what is going on and how easy it is to work in your programming language. In Smalltalk, it's often just as easy to write the code as it is to think with the diagrams. With C++, the diagrams are more useful.

The diagrams don't have to be works of art. I usually sketch them out on a paper pad or a small whiteboard. I transfer them to a drawing tool (or CASE tool) only if I think it's worth the effort of keeping them up to date because they help clarify the behavior of the classes. At this point in a project, I might also use CRC cards (see page 64) in addition to or instead of the diagrams I've been describing in this chapter.

Moving to Code

Now we can take a look at some of the code that implements the ideas I discussed in the previous sections. I'll begin with Phenomenon Type and Phenomenon since they are quite closely linked.

The first thing to think about is the association between them: Should the interface allow navigability in both directions? In this case, I think so because both directions will be valuable and they are closely linked concepts, in any case. Indeed, I am happy to implement the association with pointers in both directions, too. I shall make it an immutable association, however, as these are objects that are set up and then left alone—they are not modified often, and when they are, we can create them again.

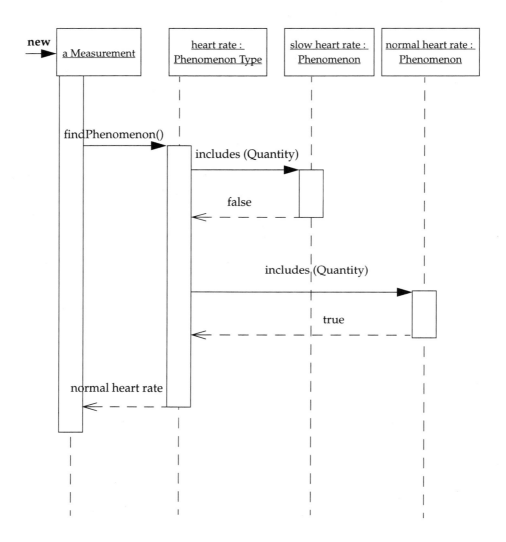

Figure 11-6: *Patient Observation Sequence Diagram*

Some people have trouble with two–way links. I don't find them troublesome if I ensure that one class takes the overall responsibility for keeping the link up to date, assisted by a "friend" or helper method, as necessary.

Let's look at some declarations.

```
public class PhenomenonType extends DomainObject {
 public PhenomenonType(String name) {
  super(name);
 };

 void friendPhenomenonAdd(Phenomenon newPhenomenon) {
  // RESTRICTED: only used by Phenomenon
  _phenomena.addElement(newPhenomenon);
 };

 public void setPhenomena(String[] names) {
  for (int i = 0; i < names.length; i++)
   new Phenomenon(names[i], this);
 };

 public Enumeration phenomena() {
  return _phenomena.elements();
 };

 private Vector _phenomena = new Vector();

 private QuantityRange _validRange;
}
```

I use the convention of adding an underscore before all fields. It helps me avoid getting my names confused.

```
public class Phenomenon extends DomainObject {
 public Phenomenon(String name, PhenomenonType type) {
  super (name);
  _type = type;
  _type.friendPhenomenonAdd(this);
 };
```

```
 public PhenomenonType phenomenonType() {
  return _type;
 };

 private PhenomenonType _type;

 private QuantityRange _range;
}


package observations;

public class DomainObject {
 public DomainObject(String name) {
  _name = name;
 };

 public DomainObject()     {};

 public String name() {
  return _name;
 };

 public String toString() {
  return _name;
 };

 protected String _name = "no name";
}
```

I've added a DomainObject class, which knows about names and will do any other behavior that I want all of my domain classes to do.

I can now set up these objects with code along the lines of the following.

```
PhenomenonType sex =
 new PhenomenonType("gender").persist();
String[] sexes = {"male", "female"};
sex.setPhenomena(sexes);
```

The **persist()** operation stores the Phenomenon Type in a registry object so that you can get it again later with a static **get()** method. I'll skip the details of that.

Next, I'll put in the code to add observations to a patient. Here I don't want all the associations to be two-way. I have the patient hang on to a collection of observations since the observations are used in the context of a patient.

```
public class Observation extends DomainObject {
 public Observation(Phenomenon relevantPhenomenon,
  Patient patient, Date whenObserved) {
   _phenomenon = relevantPhenomenon;
   patient.observationsAdd(this);
   _whenObserved = whenObserved;
 };

 private Phenomenon _phenomenon;

 private Date _whenObserved;
}


public class Patient extends DomainObject {
 public Patient(String name) {
  super(name);
 };

 void observationsAdd(Observation newObs) {
  _observations.addElement(newObs);
 };

 private Vector _observations = new Vector();
}
```

With this I can create observations.

```
new Patient("Adams").persist();
new Observation(PhenomenonType.get("gender").
 phenomenonNamed("male"), Patient.get("Adams"),
 new Date (96, 3, 1) );
```

```
class PhenomenonType {
 public Phenomenon phenomenonNamed(String name) {
  Enumeration e = phenomena();
  while (e.hasMoreElements() )
  {
   Phenomenon each = (Phenomenon)e.nextElement();
   if (each.name() == name)
    return each;
  };

  return null;
 }
```

After creating observations, I need to be able to find the latest phenomenon.

```
class Patient
 public Phenomenon phenomenonOf
  (PhenomenonType phenomenonType)
 {
  return (latestObservation(phenomenonType) ==
   null ? new NullPhenomenon() :
   latestObservation(phenomenonType).phenomenon() );
 }

 private Observation
  latestObservation(PhenomenonType value) {
  return latestObservationIn(observationsOf(value) );
 }

 private Enumeration
  observationsOf(PhenomenonType value) {
   Vector result = new Vector();
   Enumeration e = observations();
   while (e.hasMoreElements() )
   {
    Observation each = (Observation) e.nextElement();
    if (each.phenomenonType() == value)
     result.addElement(each);
   };
  return result.elements();
 }
```

```
 private Observation latestObservationIn
   (Enumeration observationEnum) {
   if (!observationEnum.hasMoreElements() )
    return null;
   Observation result =
    (Observation)observationEnum.nextElement();
   if (!observationEnum.hasMoreElements() )
    return result;

   do
   {
    Observation each =
     (Observation)observationEnum.nextElement();
    if (each.whenObserved().
     after(result.whenObserved() ) )
      result = each;
   }

   while (observationEnum.hasMoreElements() );

   return result;
 }

class Observation
 public PhenomenonType phenomenonType() {
  return _phenomenon.phenomenonType();
 }
```

There are several methods that combine to do this. You could draw a
diagram to show this, but I tend not to bother. The way I decompose a
method has more to do with refactoring (see page 30) than it does with
prior design.

We can now look at adding the behavior for measurements.

First, let's see the definition of the Measurement class and its constructor.

```
public class Measurement extends Observation {
 public Measurement(Quantity amount,
  PhenomenonType phenomenonType,
  Patient patient, Date whenObserved) {
   initialize (patient, whenObserved);
```

```
  _amount = amount;
  _phenomenonType = phenomenonType;
};

public PhenomenonType phenomenonType() {
 return _phenomenonType;
};

public String toString() {
 return _phenomenonType + ": " + _amount;
};

private Quantity _amount;

private PhenomenonType _phenomenonType;
}


class Observation
 protected void initialize(Patient patient,
  Date whenObserved) {
   patient.observationsAdd(this);
   _whenObserved = whenObserved;
 }
```

Note that a class diagram gives us a good start on developing this.

We again need the latest measurement.

```
Class Patient
 public Quantity latestAmountOf(PhenomenonType value) {
  return ((latestMeasurement(value) == null) ) ?
  new NullQuantity():latestMeasurement(value).amount();
 }

 private Measurement
  latestMeasurement(PhenomenonType value) {
   if (latestObservation(value) == null)
    return null;
   if (!latestObservation(value).isMeasurement() )
    return null;
   return (Measurement)latestObservation(value);
 }
```

In both of these cases, the class diagram suggests basic structure and we add behavior to it to support more interesting queries.

At this stage, we could describe our position with the specification-perspective class diagram shown in Figure 11-7.

Take a look at how this diagram stresses interface over implementation. I've modeled the role from Phenomenon Type to Phenomenon as a qualified role because that's the primary interface on Phenomenon Type. Similarly, I've shown Observation with a link to Phenomenon Type because the interface exists there, even though the measurement is the only one with a direct pointer to Phenomenon.

Looking at this diagram, we can see that the only difference between Measurement and Observation is that Measurement has a quantity. We could remove the Measurement class entirely from the specification model by allowing any observation to have a (potentially null) quantity.

We could still have a separate Measurement class, which would have *amount* and *phenomenon type* fields, but nobody outside the package would be aware of the class's existence. We would need to add Factory methods (Gamma *et al.* 1994) either on Observation or on Patient to allow the appropriate class to be created.

I will leave that change as an exercise for the reader and move on to assigning a Phenomenon automatically for a Measurement.

Figure 11-7 illustrates the general process.

First, we need to add a method call to Measurement's constructor.

```
Class Measurement
  public Measurement (Quantity amount,
  PhenomenonType phenomenonType,
  Patient patient, Date whenObserved)
    initialize (patient, whenObserved);
   _amount = amount;
   _phenomenonType = phenomenonType;
   _phenomenon =  calculatePhenomenonFor(_amount);
```

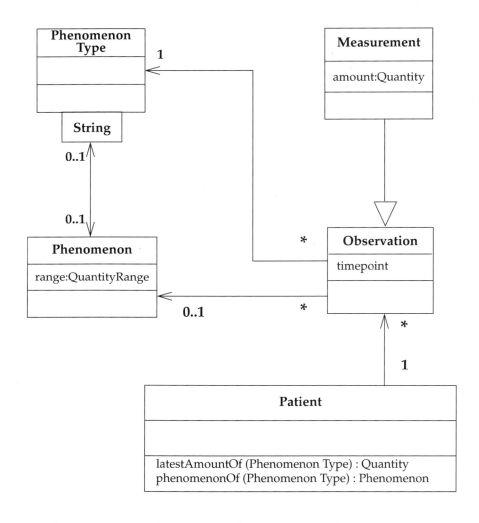

Figure 11-7: *Another Patient Observation Specification Model*

This delegates the task to Phenomenon Type.

```
Class Measurement
 public Phenomenon calculatePhenomenonFor(Quantity arg)
 {
  return _phenomenonType.phenomenonIncluding(arg);
 }
```

This asks each phenomenon in turn.

```
Class PhenomenonType
  public Phenomenon phenomenonIncluding (Quantity arg) {
   Enumeration e = phenomena();
   while (e.hasMoreElements())
   {
    Phenomenon each = (Phenomenon) e.nextElement();
    if (each.includes(arg))
     return each;
   };

   return null;
  }
Class Phenomenon
  public boolean includes (Quantity arg) {
   return (_range == null ? false:_range.includes(arg));
  }
```

The code flows out well from the sequence diagram. In practice, I usually use a sequence diagram to rough out the interaction and then make some changes as I code it. If the interaction is important, I will update the sequence chart as part of my documentation. If I think the sequence chart will not add much clarity to the code, I file the rough sequence chart in the circular filing cabinet.

This is a brief example of how to use the UML with a programming language, but it should give you a good idea of the process. You don't have to be on a high-ceremony project to find using bits of the UML handy. You don't have to use all of it, just the bits you like.

Sketching out a design with a class diagram and an interaction diagram can help get your thoughts in order and make it easier to code. I think of these sketches as fast prototypes. You don't have to hold on to the diagrams later, but you may find it easier for yourself and others to understand the code if you do.

You don't need a fancy and expensive CASE tool. A whiteboard and a simple drawing tool on your computer will do fine. Of course there are useful CASE tools, and if you are involved in a larger project, you might consider getting one.

If you do, compare it to the baseline of a simple drawing tool and a word processor (it's amazing how much you can do with Visio and Word, for instance). If the tool has code generation, look carefully at how it generates code. Code generation forces the CASE tool to take a very particular interpretation of the diagrams, which will affect the way you draw the diagrams and what the diagrams mean.

I've done medium-size projects in which we started with a CASE tool and ended up throwing it away. Don't be afraid to do that if you find the tool isn't helping.

You can find more about this example at my Web site (<**our-world.compuserve.com/homepages/Martin_Fowler**>). The version of the example at the site goes more deeply into some of the layering issues involved in getting this model to a user interface.

Appendix A

Techniques and Their Uses

Technique	Purpose
Activity Diagram	Shows behavior with control structure. Can show many objects over many uses, many objects in single use case, or implementation of method. Encourages parallel behavior.
Class Diagram	Shows static structure of concepts, types, and classes. Concepts show how users think about the world; types show interfaces of software components; classes show implementation of software components.
CRC Cards	Helps get to essence of class's purpose. Good for exploring how to implement use case. Use if getting bogged down with details or if learning object approach to design.
Deployment Diagram	Shows physical layout of components on hardware nodes.

Technique	*Purpose*
Design by Contract	Provides rigorous definition of operation's purpose and class's legal state. Encode these in class to enhance debugging.
Interaction Diagram	Shows how several objects collaborate in single use case.
Package Diagram	Shows groups of classes and dependencies among them.
Patterns	Offers useful bits of analysis, design, and coding techniques. Good examples to learn from; starting point for designs.
Refactoring	Helps in making changes to working program to improve structure. Use when code is getting in the way of good design.
State Diagram	Shows how single object behaves across many use cases.
Use Case	Elicits requirements from users in meaningful chunks. Construction planning is built around delivering some use cases in each iteration. Basis for system testing.

Appendix B

Changes from UML 1.0 to 1.1

September 1997 saw the release of UML 1.1, which incorporates many changes resulting from the OMG standardization process. Copies of *UML Distilled* from the sixth printing onwards will be adjusted for these changes. However, for those of you with earlier printings of this book, I have put together this document to summarize changes. I'm not going to discuss all the changes from UML 1.0 to 1.1, but rather only those that

- change something I said in *UML Distilled*, or
- represent important features that I would have discussed in *UML Distilled*

Be aware that there is a painful version numbering problem. When the new version of UML was released, it was called 1.1, as it followed from 1.0; quite logical. This logic was then defeated as the OMG adopted the standard and called it version 1.0. So, UML version 1.1 is OMG UML version 1.0, which is different than the original version 1.0. Are you confused yet?

I am continuing to follow the spirit of *UML Distilled*: to discuss the key elements of UML as they affect the application of the UML within real world projects. As ever, the selections and advice are my own. If there is any conflict between what I say and the official UML documents, the UML documents are the ones to follow. (But do let me know, so I can make corrections.)

I have also taken the opportunity to indicate any important errors or omissions. Thanks to the readers who have pointed these out to me.

Type and Implementation Class

On page 55 of *UML Distilled*, I talked about perspectives, and how they altered the way people draw and interpret models, in particular class diagrams. UML now takes this into account by saying that all classes on a class diagram can be specialized as either types or implementation classes.

An **implementation class** corresponds to a class in the software environment in which you are developing. A **type** is rather more nebulous; it represents a less implementation-bound abstraction. This could be a CORBA type, a specification perspective of a class, or a conceptual perspective. If necessary, you can add stereotypes to differentiate further.

You can state that for a particular diagram, all classes follow a particular stereotype. This is what you would do when drawing a diagram from a particular perspective. The implementation perspective would use implementation classes, while the specification and conceptual perspective would use types.

You use the realization relationship to indicate that an implementation class implements one or more types.

There is a distinction between type and interface. An interface is intended to directly correspond to a Java or COM style interface. Interfaces thus have only operations and no attributes.

You may use only single, static classification with implementation classes, but you can use multiple and dynamic classification with types. (I assume this is because the major OO languages follow single, static classification. If one fine day you use a language that supports multiple or dynamic classification, that restriction really should not apply.)

Class Scope Operations and Attributes

UML refers to an operation or attribute that applies to the class, rather than an instance, as having **class scope**. This is equivalent to static members in C++ or Java and to class variables and methods in Small-talk. Class scope features are <u>underlined</u> on a class diagram. This notation was available in UML 1.0, but I neglected to discuss it.

Complete and Incomplete Discriminator Constraints

On page 78 of previous printings of *UML Distilled*, I said that the {complete} constraint on a generalization indicated that all instances of the supertype must also be an instance of a subtype within that partition. UML 1.1 defines instead that {complete} indicates that all subtypes within that partition have been specified, which is not quite the same thing. In conversations, I have found some inconsistency on the interpretation of this constraint, so you should be wary of it. If you do want to indicate that all instances of the supertype should be an instance of one of the subtypes, then I suggest using another constraint to avoid confusion. Currently, I am using {mandatory}.

Composition

In UML 1.0, using composition implied that the link was immutable (or frozen; see below), at least for single-valued components. That constraint is no longer part of the definition. To be fair, there is still some confusion over the interpretation of this.

Immutability

UML defines the constraint {frozen} to define immutability on association roles. As it's currently defined, it doesn't seem to apply it to attributes or classes. In my practice, I now use the term frozen instead of immutability, and I'm happy to apply the constraint to association roles, classes, and attributes.

Returns on Sequence Diagrams

In UML 1.0, a return on a sequence diagram was distinguished by using a stick arrowhead instead of a solid arrowhead (see page 104). This was something of a pain, since the distinction was too subtle and easy to miss. UML 1.1 uses a dashed arrow for a return, which pleases me, as it makes returns much more obvious. (Since I used dashed returns in *Analysis Patterns*, it also makes me look influential.) You can name what is returned for later use by using the form "enoughStock := check()".

Use of the Term "Role"

In UML 1.0, the term **role** primarily indicated a direction on an association (see page 57). UML 1.1 refers to this usage as an **association role**. There is also a **collaboration role**, which is a role that an instance of a class plays in a collaboration. UML 1.1 gives a lot more emphasis to collaborations, and it looks like this usage of "role" will become the primary one.

Iteration Markers

In both UML 1.0 and 1.1, you can use a * to mark messages that occur many times on a Sequence Diagram, Collaboration Diagram, or Activity Diagram. Often it is useful to indicate what the basis of the iteration is. You can do this by using an expression within []: for example, *[for all line items], or *[i=1..n]. (UML does not prescribe what the contents of expression are—use either English or your programming language.)

Bibliography

Kent Beck: *Smalltalk Best Practice Patterns*. Prentice Hall, 1996.

Kent Beck: "Make It Run, Make It Right: Design Through Refactoring." *The Smalltalk Report*, Vol. 6, No. 4, pp. 19-24, SIGS Publications, January 1997.

Kent Beck and Ward Cunningham: "A Laboratory For Teaching Object-Oriented Thinking." *Proceedings of OOPSLA 89*. SIGPLAN Notices, Vol. 24, No. 10, pp. 1-6. See **<http://c2.com/doc/oopsla89/ paper.html>**

Grady Booch: *Object-Oriented Analysis and Design with Applications, Second Edition*. Addison-Wesley, 1994.

Grady Booch: *Object Solutions: Managing the Object-Oriented Project*. Addison-Wesley, 1996.

Frank Buschmann, Regine Meunier, Hans Rohnert, Peter Sommerlad, and Michael Stal: *Pattern-Oriented Software Architecture: A System of Patterns*. John Wiley & Sons, 1996.

Peter Coad and Jill Nicola: *Object-Oriented Programming*. Yourdon, 1993.

Peter Coad, David North, and Mark Mayfield: *Object Models: Strategies, Patterns and Applications*. Prentice Hall, 1995.

Peter Coad and Edward Yourdon: *Object-Oriented Analysis*. Yourdon, 1991.

Peter Coad and Edward Yourdon: *Object-Oriented Design*. Yourdon, 1991.

Steve Cook and John Daniels: *Designing Object Systems: Object-Oriented Modeling with Syntropy*. Prentice Hall, 1994.

James Coplien: "A Generative Development Process Pattern Language." In Coplien and Schmidt, 1995, pp. 183-237.

James O. Coplien and Douglas C. Schmidt, eds.: *Pattern Languages of Program Design* [PLoPD1]. Addison-Wesley, 1995.

Ward Cunningham: "EPISODES: A Pattern Language of Competitive Development." In Vlissides *et al.* 1996, pp. 371-388.

Martin Fowler: *Analysis Patterns: Reusable Object Models*. Addison-Wesley, 1997.

Erich Gamma, Richard Helm, Ralph Johnson, and John Vlissides [Gang of Four]: *Design Patterns: Elements of Reusable Object-Oriented Software*. Addison-Wesley, 1995.

Adele Goldberg and Kenneth S. Rubin: *Succeeding With Objects: Decision Frameworks for Project Management*. Addison-Wesley, 1995.

Ian Graham: *Object-Oriented Methods, Second Edition*. Addison-Wesley, 1994.

David Harel: "Statecharts: A Visual Formalism for Complex Systems." In *Science of Computer Programming*, Vol. 8, 1987.

Ivar Jacobson, Magnus Christerson, Patrik Jonsson, and Gunnar Övergaard: *Object-Oriented Software Engineering: A Use Case Driven Approach*. Addison-Wesley, 1992.

Ivar Jacobson, Maria Ericsson, and Agneta Jacobson: *The Object Advantage: Business Process Reengineering with Object Technology*. Addison-Wesley, 1995.

Andrew Koenig and Barbara Moo: *Ruminations on C++: A Decade of Programming Insight and Experience*. Addison-Wesley, 1997.

James Martin and James J. Odell: *Object-Oriented Methods: A Foundation*. Prentice Hall, 1994.

James Martin and James J. Odell: *Object-Oriented Methods: Pragmatic Considerations*. Prentice Hall, 1996.

Robert Cecil Martin: *Designing Object-Oriented C++ Applications: Using the Booch Method*. Prentice Hall, 1995.

Steve McConnell: *Rapid Development: Taming Wild Software Schedules.* Microsoft Press, 1996.

Bertrand Meyer: *Object-Oriented Software Construction.* Prentice Hall, 1997.

William F. Opdyke: *Refactoring Object-Oriented Frameworks.* Ph.D. Thesis, University of Illinois at Urbana-Champaign, 1992. See <**ftp:// st.cs.uiuc.edu/pub/papers/refactoring/opdyke-thesis.ps.Z**>

James Rumbaugh: *OMT Insights.* SIGS Books, 1996.

James Rumbaugh, Michael Blaha, William Premerlani, Frederick Eddy, and William Lorenzen: *Object-Oriented Modeling and Design.* Prentice Hall, 1991.

Sally Shlaer and Stephen J. Mellor: *Object Lifecycles: Modeling the World in States.* Yourdon, 1991.

Sally Shlaer and Stephen J. Mellor: *Object-Oriented Systems Analysis: Modeling the World in Data.* Yourdon, 1989.

Sally Shlaer and Stephen J. Mellor: "Recursive Design of an Application Independent Architecture." *IEEE Software*, Vol. 14, No. 1, 1997.

John M. Vlissides, James O. Coplien, and Norman L. Kerth, eds.: *Pattern Languages of Program Design 2* [PLoPD2]. Addison-Wesley, 1996.

Kim Walden and Jean-Marc Nerson: *Seamless Object-Oriented Software Architecture: Analysis and Design of Reliable Systems.* Prentice Hall, 1995.

Rebecca Wirfs-Brock, Brian Wilkerson, and Lauren Wiener: *Designing Object-Oriented Software.* Prentice Hall, 1990.

Index

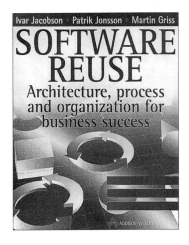

Software Reuse
*Architecture, Process, and Organization
for Business Success*
Ivar Jacobson, Martin Griss, Patrik Jonsson
Addison-Wesley Object Technology Series

This long-awaited book brings software engineers, designers, programmers, and their managers a giant step closer to a future in which object-oriented component-based software engineering is the norm. Jacobson, Griss, and Jonsson develop a coherent model and set of guidelines for ensuring success with large-scale, systematic, OO reuse. Their framework, referred to as "Reuse-Driven Software Engineering Business" (Reuse Business) deals systematically with the key business process, architecture, and organization issues that hinder success with reuse.

0-201-92476-5   Hardcover   560 pages   ©1997

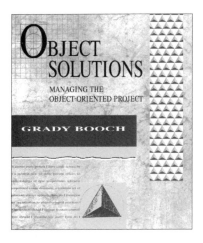

Object Solutions
Managing the Object-Oriented Project
Grady Booch
Addison-Wesley Object Technology Series

Object Solutions is a direct outgrowth of Grady Booch's experience with object-oriented projects in development around the world. This book focuses on the development process and is the perfect resource for developers and managers who want to implement object technologies for the first time or refine their existing object-oriented development practice. The book is divided into two major sections. The first four chapters describe in detail the process of object-oriented development in terms of inputs, outputs, products, activities, and milestones. The remaining ten chapters provide practical advice on key issues including management, planning, reuse, and quality assurance. Drawing upon his knowledge of strategies used in both successful and unsuccessful projects, Grady Booch offers pragmatic advice for applying object technologies and controlling projects effectively.

0-8053-0594-7   Paperback   336 pages   ©1996

The CRC Card Book
David Bellin and Susan Suchman Simone
Forewords by Kent Beck and Ward Cunningham
Addison-Wesley Object Technology Series

CRC cards help project teams "act out" the various parts of a problem domain. The application developer can use these cards to define the Classes, the Relationships between classes, and the Collaboration between these classes (CRC) prior to beginning the OO design of the application program. The case studies in this book are presented in the engaging style of a novella to demonstrate how personalities and organizational culture come into play when using the CRC technique. C++, Java, and Smalltalk experts provide implementation examples in each language. This book demonstrates how to discover classes through team brainstorming, manage an object-oriented project, refine project requirements, test the conception of the system, and evaluate potential paths of collaboration using role play.

0-201-89535-8   Paperback   320 pages   ©1997

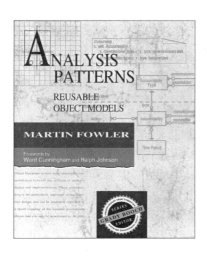

Analysis Patterns
Reusable Object Models
Martin Fowler

"In his long-awaited book, Martin Fowler has done for application domain patterns what the Gang of Four [Gamma et al.] have done for general purpose design patterns in their book, Design Patterns: Elements of Reusable Object-Oriented Software. *This book is a must have for all analysts and designers doing object-oriented business modeling and business process re-engineering."*
        —Donald G. Firesmith,
            Knowledge Systems Corporation

Fowler shares with you his wealth of object modeling experience and his keen eye for identifying repeating problems and transforming them into reusable models. *Analysis Patterns* provides a catalogue of patterns that have emerged in a wide range of domains, including trading, measurement, accounting, and organizational relationships.

0-201-89542-0   Hardcover   672 pages   ©1997

Addison-Wesley is pleased to announce the signing of Grady Booch, Ivar Jacobson, and James Rumbaugh, the creators of the Unified Modeling Language (UML), to write the definitive reference books on the UML. These books continue the tradition of excellence in object technology publishing for which Addison-Wesley is known.

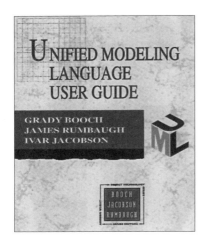

Unified Modeling Language User Guide

Grady Booch, James Rumbaugh, Ivar Jacobson
Addison-Wesley Object Technology Series

The *Unified Modeling Language User Guide* is the first of two definitive UML works written by Grady Booch, James Rumbaugh, and Ivar Jacobson. This book will introduce the core eighty percent of the UML, approaching it in a layered fashion and showing the application of the UML to modeling problems found across a variety of application domains. The *Unified Modeling Language User Guide* is suitable for developers unfamiliar with the UML or with modeling in general, but will also be useful to advanced developers who wish to learn how to apply the UML to advanced problems.

0-201-57168-4   Paperback   320 pages   ©1999
Available Fall 1998

Unified Modeling Language Reference Manual

James Rumbaugh, Grady Booch, Ivar Jacobson
Addison-Wesley Object Technology Series

James Rumbaugh, Ivar Jacobson, and Grady Booch have created the definitive reference to the UML. The book covers every aspect and detail of the UML and presents the language in a useful reference format that every serious software architect or programmer will need on his bookshelf. The book is organized by topic and designed for quick access. The authors also provide the necessary information to enable existing OMT, Booch, and OOSE notation users to make the transition to the UML. The book provides an overview of the semantic foundation of the UML through a concise appendix.

0-201-30998-X   Paperback   480 pages   ©1999
Available Winter 1998

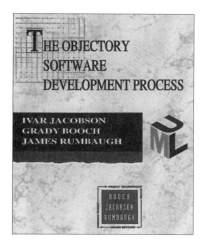

The Objectory Software Development Process
Ivar Jacobson, Grady Booch, James Rumbaugh
Addison-Wesley Object Technology Series

The Objectory Software Development Process is a component-based, use case–driven, architecture-centered, iterative, and incremental developmental process that uses the Unified Modeling Language to represent models of the software system to be developed. The Objectory Process brings together the best aspects of the OMT, Booch, and OOSE (use case) methodologies along with insights from other methods to create a strong candidate for a standard software analysis and design process. This third book from Ivar Jacobson, Grady Booch, and James Rumbaugh serves as the definitive reference to this important new process. This book describes the different models developed during the life-cycle of a system, and it explains the different higher-level constructs—notations as well as semantics—used in the models. Thus stereotypes such as use cases and actors, packages, classes, stereotypes, interfaces, active classes, processes and threads, nodes, and most relations will be described intuitively in the context of a model. The book includes one ongoing example that illustrates the application of the process in all phases of the product development life-cycle.

0-201-57169-2   Hardcover   352 pages   ©1999
Available Winter 1998

Inside CORBA
Distributed Object Standards and Applications
Thomas Mowbray and William Ruh
Addison-Wesley Object Technology Series

Inside CORBA is a comprehensive, up-to-date, and authoritative guide to distributed object architecture, software development, and CORBA standards. It includes the latest coverage of the new CORBA IDL Language Mapping for the Java programming language and comprehensive coverage of the CORBA 2 standard and CORBA services. This newest CORBA book is a "must read" for all managers, architects, and developers building distributed systems. The authors outline essential lessons learned from experienced CORBA managers and architects to ensure successful adoption and migration to CORBA technology. Also included is the first comprehensive architectural model of CORBA components and services designed to support rapid understanding of complex OMG standards and their interrelationships.

0-201-89540-4   Paperback   352 pages   ©1997

Package Diagram

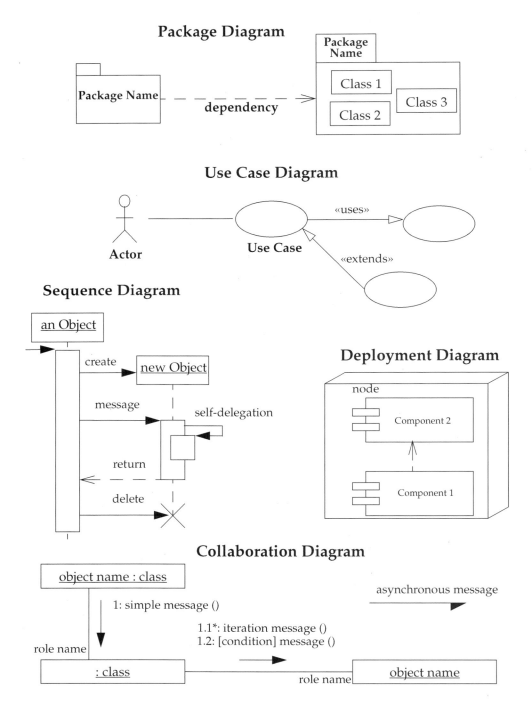

Package Name

Package Name

dependency

Class 1

Class 2

Class 3

Use Case Diagram

Actor

Use Case

«uses»

«extends»

Sequence Diagram

an Object

create

new Object

message

self-delegation

return

delete

Deployment Diagram

node

Component 2

Component 1

Collaboration Diagram

object name : class

1: simple message ()

1.1*: iteration message ()
1.2: [condition] message ()

asynchronous message

role name

: class

role name

object name